Execution of Justice

by Emily Mann

A Samuel French Acting Edition

SAMUELFRENCH.COM

Copyright © 1983, 1985, 1986 by Emily Mann
ALL RIGHTS RESERVED

CAUTION: Professionals and amateurs are hereby warned that *EXECUTION OF JUSTICE* is subject to a licensing fee. It is fully protected under the copyright laws of the United States of America, the British Commonwealth, including Canada, and all other countries of the Copyright Union. All rights, including professional, amateur, motion picture, recitation, lecturing, public reading, radio broadcasting, television and the rights of translation into foreign languages are strictly reserved. In its present form the play is dedicated to the reading public only.

The amateur and professional live stage performance rights to *EXECUTION OF JUSTICE* are controlled exclusively by Samuel French, Inc., and licensing arrangements and performance licenses must be secured well in advance of presentation. PLEASE NOTE that amateur licensing fees are set upon application in accordance with your producing circumstances. When applying for a licensing quotation and a performance license please give us the number of performances intended, dates of production, your seating capacity and admission fee. Licensing fees are payable one week before the opening performance of the play to Samuel French, Inc., at 45 W. 25th Street, New York, NY 10010.

Licensing fee of the required amount must be paid whether the play is presented for charity or gain and whether or not admission is charged.

Professional/Stock licensing fees quoted upon application to Samuel French, Inc.

For all other rights than those stipulated above, apply to: George P. Lane, William Morris Agency, Inc., 1350 Avenue of the Americas, New York, NY 1019.

Particular emphasis is laid on the question of amateur or professional readings, permission and terms for which must be secured in writing from Samuel French, Inc.

Copying from this book in whole or in part is strictly forbidden by law, and the right of performance is not transferable.

Whenever the play is produced the following notice must appear on all programs, printing and advertising for the play: "Produced by special arrangement with Samuel French, Inc."

Due authorship credit must be given on all programs, printing and advertising for the play.

ISBN 978-0-573-69002-0   Printed in U.S.A.   #7072

> No one shall commit or authorize any act or omission by which the copyright of, or the right to copyright, this play may be impaired.

> No one shall make any changes in this play for the purpose of production.

> Publication of this play does not imply availability for performance. Both amateurs and professionals considering a production are strongly advised in their own interests to apply to Samuel French, Inc., for written permission before starting rehearsals, advertising, or booking a theatre.

> No part of this book may be reproduced, stored in a retrieval system, or transmitted in any form, by any means, now known or yet to be invented, including mechanical, electronic, photocopying, recording, videotaping, or otherwise, without the prior written permission of the publisher.

MUSIC USE NOTE

Licensees are solely responsible for obtaining formal written permission from copyright owners to use copyrighted music in the performance of this play and are strongly cautioned to do so. If no such permission is obtained by the licensee, then the licensee must use only original music that the licensee owns and controls. Licensees are solely responsible and liable for all music clearances and shall indemnify the copyright owners of the play and their licensing agent, Samuel French, Inc., against any costs, expenses, losses and liabilities arising from the use of music by licensees.

IMPORTANT BILLING AND CREDIT REQUIREMENTS

All producers of *EXECUTION OF JUSTICE* must give credit to the Author of the Play in all programs distributed in connection with performances of the Play, and in all instances in which the title of the Play appears for the purposes of advertising, publicizing or otherwise exploiting the Play and/or a production. The name of the Author *must* appear on a separate line on which no other name appears, immediately following the title and *must* appear in size of type not less than fifty percent of the size of the title type.

In addition the following credit *must* be given in all programs and publicity information distributed in association with this piece:

> *EXECUTION OF JUSTICE* was presented on Broadway by Lester and Marjorie Ostermanand Mortimer Caplin in Association with Norton & Stark, Inc.
>
> Professional Premiere at the Actors Theatre of Louisville.
>
> Originally commissioned by the Eureka Theatre Company, San Francisco.

ⓙ VIRGINIA THEATRE

OWNED AND OPERATED BY JUJAMCYN THEATERS
RICHARD G. WOLFF, PRESIDENT

LESTER and MARJORIE   MORTIMER
    OSTERMAN   CAPLIN

and

RICHARD C. NORTON and CHRISTOPHER STARK

present

Set by   Costumes Designed by   Lighting Designed by
MING CHO   **JENNIFER**   **PAT**
LEE   **VON MAYRHAUSER**   **COLLINS**

Film sequences excerpted from THE TIMES OF HARVEY MILK
by Robert Epstein and Richard Schmiechen

Sound Designed by   Casting   General Manager   Production Stage Manager
TOM   **JOHNSON-LIFF**   **ALLAN**   **FRANK**
MORSE   **ASSOCIATES**   **FRANCIS**   **MARINO**

Written and Directed by
EMILY MANN

Originally commissioned by the Eureka Theatre Company, San Francisco.
Professional premiere at the Actors Theatre of Louisville.
Special thanks to Douglas C. Wager, Guy Bergquist and the Arena Stage for
their invaluable assistance in the development of the audio and video.

The Producers and Theatre Management are Members
of The League of New York Theatres and Producers, Inc.

CAST

DAN WHITE — John Spencer
MARY ANN WHITE — Mary McDonnell
COP — Stanley Tucci
SISTER BOOM BOOM — Wesley Snipes

CHORUS OF UNCALLED WITNESSES:
JIM DENMAN, White's Jailer — Christopher McHale
YOUNG MOTHER — Lisabeth Bartlett
MILK'S FRIEND — Adam Redfield
GWENN CRAIG, Vice President of Harvey Milk Democratic Club — Isabell Monk
City Supervisor HARRY BRITT, Milk's Successor — Donal Donnelly
JOSEPH FREITAS, D.A. — Nicholas Hormann
MOURNER — Nicholas Hormann

TRIAL CHARACTERS:
THE COURT — Nicholas Kepros
COURT CLERK — Lisabeth Bartlett
DOUGLAS SCHMIDT, Defense Atorney — Peter Friedman
THOMAS F. NORMAN, Prosecuting Attorney — Gerry Bamman
JOANNA LU, TV Reporter — Freda Foh Shen
PROSPECTIVE JURORS — Josh Clark, Suzy Hunt
JUROR #3/FOREMAN — Gary Reineke
BAILIFF — Jeremy O. Caplin

WITNESSES FOR THE PEOPLE:
CORONER STEPHENS — Donal Donnelly
RUDY NOTHENBERG, Deputy Mayor, Moscone's Friend — Earle Hyman
BARBARA TAYLOR, Reporter — Marcia Jean Kurtz
OFFICER BYRNE, Department Of Records — Isabell Monk
WILLIAM MELIA, Civil Engineer — Richard Riehle
CYR COPERTINI, Secretary To The Mayor — Suzy Hunt
CARL HENRY CARLSON, Aide To Harvey Milk — Nicholas Hormann
RICHARD PABICH, Assistant To Harvey Milk — Wesley Snipes

NOTE: The play can be performed by as few as 18 actors.

Inspector FRANK FALZON, Homicide	Jon DeVries
Inspector EDWARD ERDELATZ	Stanley Tucci

WITNESSES FOR THE DEFENSE:

DENISE APCAR, Aide To White	Lisabeth Bartlett
Fire Chief SHERRATT	Gary Reineke
Fireman FREDIANI	Jeremy O. Caplin
Police Officer SULLIVAN	Stanley Tucci
City Supervisor LEE DOLSON	Richard Riehle
Psychiatrists: DR. JONES	Earle Hyman
DR. SOLOMON	Marcia Jean Kurtz
DR. BLINDER	Donal Donnelly
DR. LUNDE	Gary Reineke
DR. DELMAN	Jon DeVries

IN REBUTTAL FOR THE PEOPLE:

City Supervisor CAROL RUTH SILVER	Marcia Jean Kurtz
DR. LEVY, Psychiatrist	Gary Reineke
RIOT POLICE	Jeremy O. Caplin, Josh Clark, Jon DeVries, Richard Riehle, Stanley Tucci
ACTION CAMERMAN	Richard Howard

UNDERSTUDIES

Understudies never substitute for listed players unless a specific announcement for the appearance is made at the time of the performance.

For Sullivan—Wesley Snipes; for Barbara Taylor—Elise Warner; for Falzon, Bailiff, Dan White, Frediani, Riot Cop, Delman—Christopher McHale; for Mary Ann White, Cyr Copertini, Juror #1, Gwenn Craig, Officer Byrne, Joanna Lu, Denise Apcar, Young Mother—Carlotta Schoch; for Sister Boom Boom, Pabich, Milk's Friend, Douglas Schmidt—Josh Clark; for Dr. Solomon, Carol Ruth Silver—Suzy Hunt; for Freitas, Carlson, Mourner—Gary Reineke; for Denman, Juror #2—Jeremy O. Caplin; for Cop, Erdelatz—Richard Riehle; for Coroner Stevens, Britt, The Court, Melia, Dolson, Riot Cop, Nothenberg, Sherratt, Foreman, Juror #3, Drs. Levy, Blinder, Jones, Lunde—Richard Poe.

THE TIME:
1978 to the present

THE PLACE:
San Francisco

THE WORDS COME FROM:
Trial Transcripts, Reportage and Interviews

EXECUTION OF JUSTICE

ACT I

MURDER

A BARE STAGE.
A WHITE SCREEN OVERHEAD.
ON SCREEN: IMAGES OF SAN FRANCISCO.
HOT, FAST MUSIC. IMAGES OF MILK AND MOSCONE
PUNCTUATE THE VISUALS.

PEOPLE ENTER. A DAY IN SAN FRANCISCO.
A MAELSTROM OF URBAN ACTIVITY.

WITHOUT WARNING: ON SCREEN: (video, if possible)

DIANNE FEINSTEIN. *(almost unable to stand)*
As President of the Board of Supervisors, It is my duty to make this announcement: Mayor George Moscone ... and Supervisor Harvey Milk ... have been shot ... and killed. *(GASPS AND CRIES. A LONG MOMENT.)* The suspect is Supervisor Dan White.

(THE CROWD IN SHOCK. THEY CANNOT MOVE. THEN THEY RUN. OUT OF THE CHAOS, DAN WHITE APPEARS.)
ON SCREEN: A CHURCH WINDOW FADES UP.
A SHAFT OF LIGHT.
DAN WHITE PRAYS.

ON AUDIO: HYPERREAL SOUNDS OF MUMBLED HAIL MARYS
SOUNDS OF A WOMAN'S HIGH HEELS ECHOING, MOVING FAST.
SOUND OF BREATHING HARD, RUNNING.
MARY ANN WHITE ENTERS, BREATHLESS.
WHITE LOOKS UP. SHE APPROACHES HIM.

WHITE. I shot the Mayor and Harvey.

(She crumples. Lights change.)

CLERK. This is the matter of the People versus Daniel James White.

(Amplified gavel. Lights change.)

COP. *(quiet)*
Yeah, I'm wearing a "Free Dan White" t-shirt. *(indicating on shirt "NO MAN IS AN ISLAND")* You haven't seen what I've seen
— my nose shoved into what I think stinks.
Against everything I believe in.
There was a time in San Francisco when you knew a guy
by his parish.

(SISTER BOOM BOOM enters.)

COP. Sometimes I sit in Church and I think of those disgusting drag queens dressed up as nuns

and I'm a cop,
and I'm thinkin',
there's gotta be a law, you know,
because they're makin' me think things I don't want to think
and I gotta keep my mouth shut.

(BOOM BOOM puts out cigarette.)

COP. Take a guy out of his sling—fist fucked to death—
they say it's mutual consent, it ain't murder,
and I pull this disgusting mess down, take him to the morgue,
I mean, my wife asks me, "Hey, how was your day?"
I can't even tell her.
I wash my hands before I can even look at my kids.

(They are very aware of each other, but possibly never make eye contact.)

BOOM BOOM.
God bless you one.
God bless you all.
 COP. See, Danny knew — he believes in the rights of minorities. Ya know, he just knew — we are a minority, too.
BOOM BOOM.
I would like to open with a reading from the Book of Dan.
(Opens book.)

COP. We been workin' this job three generations — my father was a cop — and then they put — Moscone, Jesus, the mayor — Jesus — Moscone put this
N-negro loving, faggot loving Chief telling us what to do—
he doesn't even come from the neighborhood,
he doesn't even come from this city!
He's tellin' us what to do in a force that knows what to do.
He makes us paint our cop cars faggot blue—
he called it "lavender gloves" for the queers,
handle 'em, treat 'em with "lavender gloves," he called it.
He's cuttin' off our balls.
The city is stinkin' with degenerates—
I mean, I'm worried about my kids, I worry about my wife,
I worry about me and how I'm feelin' mad all the time.
You gotta understand that I'm not alone—
It's real confusion.

BOOM BOOM. "As Dan came to his day of reckoning, he feared not for he went unto the lawyers and the doctors and the jurors, and they said, 'Take heart, for in this you will receive not life but three to seven with time off for good behavior.' " *(Closes book reverently.)*

COP. Take a walk with me sometime.
See what I see every day...
Like   I'm supposed to smile when I see two bald-headed,
shaved-head men with those tight pants and muscles,

chains everywhere, French-kissin' on the street,
putting their hands all over each other's asses,
I'm supposed to smile,
walk by, act as if this is RIGHT??!!

BOOM BOOM. As gay people and as people of color and as women we all know the cycle of brutality and ignorance which pervades our culture.

COP. I got nothin' against people doin' what they want,
if I don't see it.

BOOM BOOM. And we all know that brutality only begets more brutality.

COP. I mean, I'm not makin' some woman on the streets for everyone to see.

BOOM BOOM. Violence only sows the seed for more violence.

COP. I'm not...

BOOM BOOM. And I hope Dan White knows that.

COP. I can't explain it any better.

BOOM BOOM. Because the greatest, most efficient information gathering and dispersal network is the Great Gay Grapevine.

COP. Just take my word for it—

BOOM BOOM. And when Dan White gets out of jail, no matter where Dan White goes, someone will recognize him.

COP. Walk into a leather bar with me some night—
They — they're—
there are queers who'd agree with me — it's disgusting.

BOOM BOOM.
All over the world, the word will go out.

And we will know where Dan White is.

COP. The point is: Dan White showed you could fight City Hall.

BOOM BOOM. *(pause)*
Now we are all aware, as I said,
Of this cycle of brutality and murder.
And the only way we can break that horrible cycle is with love, understanding and forgiveness.
And there are those who were before me here today—
gay brothers and sisters
who said that we must somehow learn to
love, understand and forgive
the sins that have been committed against us
and the sins of violence
And it sort of grieves me that some of us are not
Understanding and loving and forgiving of Dan White.
And after he gets out,
after we find out where he is...
(Long, wry look.)
I mean, not, y'know,
with any malice or planning...
(Long look.)
You know, you get so depressed and your blood sugar goes up
and you'd be capable of just about *ANYTHING!*
(Long pause. Smiles.)
And some angry faggot or dyke who is not
understanding, loving and forgiving—
is going to perform a horrible act of violence and brutality

against Dan White.
And if we can't break the cycle before somebody gets Dan White
somebody will *get Dan White.*
and when they do,
I beg you all to
love, understand and *for-give. (He throws a kiss, laughs.)*

(Lights fade to black.)

CLERK. This is the matter of the People vs. Daniel James White and the record will show that the Defendant is present with his counsel and the District Attorney is present and this is out of presence of the jury.

(Court setting up. TV lights.)

JOANNA LU. *(On camera.)* The list of prospective witnesses that the defense has presented for the trial of the man accused of killing the liberal Mayor of San Francisco, George Moscone, and the first avowedly homosexual elected official, City Supervisor Harvey Milk, reads like a Who's Who of City Government
(Looks at list.)
...Judges, Congressmen, current and former Supervisors, and even a State Senator. The D.A. has charged White with two counts of first degree murder, invoking for the first time the clause in the new California capital punishment law that calls for the gas chamber for any person who has assassinated a public official in an attempt to prevent him from fulfilling his official duties.

Ironically, Harvey Milk and George Moscone vigorously lobbied against the death penalty while Dan White vigorously supported it. This is Joanna Lu at the Hall of Justice.

(Gavel. Spotlight on clerk.)

CLERK. Ladies and gentlemen, this is the information in the case now pending before you: the People of the State of California, Plaintiff, versus Daniel James White, Defendant. Action Number: 98663, Count One.

(Gavel.)
(Lights.)
(On screen: JURY SELECTION.)

COURT. Mr. Schmidt, you may continue with your jury selection.
SCHMIDT. Thank you, Your Honor.
CLERK. It is alleged that Daniel James White did willfully unlawfully and with malice aforethought murder George R. Moscone, the duly elected Mayor of the City and County of San Francisco, California.
SCHMIDT. Have you ever supported controversial causes, like homosexual rights, for instance?
JUROR #1. *(woman)* I have gay friends...I, uh...once walked with them in a Gay Freedom Day Parade.
SCHMIDT. Your Honor, I would like to strike the juror.
JUROR #1. *(woman)* I am str...I am heterosexual.
COURT. Agreed.

(Gavel.)

CLERK. The defendant Daniel James White is further accused of a crime of felony to wit: that said defendant Daniel James White did willfully, unlawfully and with malice aforethought, murder Harvey Milk, a duly elected Supervisor of the City and County of San Francisco, California.

SCHMIDT. With whom do you live, sir?

JUROR #2. *(man)* My roommate.

SCHMIDT. What does he or she do?

JUROR #2. *(man)* He works at the Holiday Inn.

SCHMIDT. Your Honor, I ask the court to strike the juror for cause.

COURT. Agreed.

(Gavel.)

CLERK. Special circumstances: it is alleged that Daniel James White in this proceeding has been accused of more than one offense of murder.

JUROR #3. I worked briefly as a San Francisco policeman, but I've spent most of my life since then as a private security guard.

SCHMIDT. As you know, serving as a juror is a high honor and responsibility.

JUROR #3. Yes, sir.

SCHMIDT. The jury serves as the conscience of the community.

JUROR #3. Yes, sir. I know that, sir.

SCHMIDT. Now, sir, as a juror you take an oath that you

will apply the laws of the State of California as the Judge will instruct you. You'll uphold that oath, won't you?

JUROR #3. Yes, sir.

SCHMIDT. Do you hold any views against the death penalty no matter how heinous the crime?

JUROR #3. No, sir. I support the death penalty.

SCHMIDT. Why do you think Danny White killed Milk and Moscone?

JUROR #3. I have certain opinions. I'd say it was social and political pressures...

SCHMIDT. I have my jury.

COURT. Mr. Norman?

(No response. Fine with him.)
(Gavel.)

JOANNA LU. *(On camera.)* The jury has been selected quickly for the Dan White trial. It appears the prosecution and the defense want the same jury. The prosecuting attorney, Assistant D.A. Tom Norman exercised only 3 out of 27 possible peremptory challenges. By all accounts, there are no Blacks, no gays, and no Asians. One juror is an ex-policeman, another the wife of the county jailer, four of the seven women are old enough to be Dan White's mother. Most of the jurors are working and middle-class Catholics. Speculation in the press box is that the prosecution feels that it has a law-and-order jury. In any case, Dan White will certainly be judged by a jury of his peers.
(Turns.)
 have with me this morning District Attorney Joseph

Freitas, Jr.
(TV lights on FREITAS.)
May we ask, sir, the prosecution's strategy in the trial of Dan White?

FREITAS. I think it's a clear case — We'll let the facts speak for themselves—

CLERK. And the Defendant, Daniel James White, has entered a plea of not guilty to each of the charges and allegations contained in this information.

(WHITE enters. MRS. WHITE enters.)

COURT. Mr. Norman, do you desire to make an opening statement at this time?
NORMAN. I do, Judge.
COURT. All right. You may proceed.

(Lights change.)
(On screen: ACT ONE MURDER.)(Gavel.)
(All screens go to white.)

NORMAN. *(Opening statement. The prosecution.)* Your Honor, members of the jury, and you must be the judges now, *(Actor takes in audience.)* counsel for the defense: *(To audience.)*
Ladies and gentlemen — I am Thomas F. Norman and I am the Assistant District Attorney, and I appear here as trial representative to Joseph Freitas Jr, District Attorney. Seated with me is Frank Falzon, Chief Inspector of Homicide for San Francisco.
George R. Moscone was the duly-elected Mayor of

San Francisco.

(On screen: Portrait of MOSCONE.)

Harvey Milk was the duly-elected Supervisor or City Councilman of District 5 of San Francisco.

(On screen: Portrait of HARVEY MILK.)

The defendant in this case, Mr. Daniel James White, had been the duly-elected Supervisor of District 8 of San Francisco, until for personal reasons of his own he tendered his resignation in writing to the Mayor on or about November the 10th, 1978, which was approximately 17 days before this tragedy occured.
Subsequent to tendering his resignation he had the feeling that he wanted to withdraw that resignation, and that he wanted his job back. George Moscone, it appears, had told the accused that he would give him his job back or, in other words, appoint him back to the Board if it appeared that there was substantial support in District Number 8 for that appointment.
Material was received by the Mayor in that regard, and in the meantime, Mr. Daniel James White had resorted to the courts in an effort to withdraw his written resignation.
It appears that those efforts were not met with much success.

(On screen: The defense, DOUGLAS SCHMIDT.)

SCHMIDT. Ladies and Gentlemen, the prosecutor has quite skillfully outlined certain of the facts that he believes will be supportive of his theory of first-degree murder.
I intend to present ALL the facts, including some of the background material that will show, not so much *what* happened on November 27th, but WHY those tragedies occured on November 27th.
The evidence will show, and it's not disputed, that Dan White did, indeed, shoot and kill George Moscone and I think the evidence is equally clear that Dan White did shoot and kill Harvey Milk.
Why then should there be a trial?
The issue in this trial is properly to understand WHY that happened.

(On screen: Chief Medical Examiner and Coroner for the City and County of San Francisco.)
(Lights.)
(Coroner sits.)

STEPHENS. *(Holding photo.)* In my opinion and experience, Counsel, the larger tattoo pattern at the side of the Mayor's head is compatible with a firing distance of about one foot, and the smaller tattoo pattern within the larger tattoo pattern is consistent with a firing distance of a little less than one foot.
That is: The wounds to the head were received within a distance of one foot when the Mayor was already on the floor incapacitated.

(NORMAN looks to jury.)
(On screen: Image of figure shooting man in head from a distance of one foot, leaning down "Coup De Grace.")

SCHMIDT. Why?...Good people, fine people, with fine backgrounds, simply don't kill people in cold blood, it just doesn't happen, and obviously some part of them has not been presented thus far. Dan White was a native of San Francisco. He went to school here, went through high school here. He was a noted athlete in high school. He was an army veteran who served in Vietnam, and was honorably discharged from the army. He became a policeman thereafter, and after a brief hiatus developed, again returned to the police force in San Francisco, and later transferred to the fire department.
He was married in December of 1976,
(HE indicates MARY ANN WHITE.)
and he fathered his son in July 1978.
Dan White was a good policeman and Dan White was a good fireman. In fact, he was decorated for having saved a woman and her child in a very dangerous fire, but the complete picture of Dan White perhaps was not known until some time after these tragedies on November 27th. The part that went unrecognized was since his early manhood, Daniel White was suffering from a mental disease. The diease that Daniel White was suffering from is called depression, sometimes called manic depression or uni-polar depression.

NORMAN. Doctor, what kind of a wound was that in your opinion?

STEPHENS. These are gunshot wounds of entrance, Counsel.

The cause of death was multiple gunshot wounds...particularly the bullet that passed through the base of the Supervisor's brain. This wound would cause instant or almost instant death. I am now holding People's 30 and 29 for identification. In order for this wound to be received, Counsel...the Supervisor's left arm has to be relatively close to the body with the palm turned away from the body and the thumb towards the body.
NORMAN. Can you illustrate that for us?
STEPHENS. Yes, Counsel. The left arm has to be in close to the body and slightly forward with the palm up. The right hand has to be palm away with the thumb pointed towards the body and the elbow in slightly to the body with the arm raised. In this position, all of these wounds that I have just described in People's 30 and 29 line up.
NORMAN. Thank you.

(Freeze on position. Lights.)

SCHMIDT. *(To jury.)* Dan White came from a vastly different lifestyle than Harvey Milk, who was a homosexual leader and politician. Dan White was an idealistic young man, a working class young man. He was deeply endowed with and believed very strongly in the traditional American values, family and home; like the District he represented.
(Indicates jury.)
Dan White believed people when they said something. He believed that a man's word, essentially, was his bond. I don't think Dan White was particularly insightful as to

what his underlying problem was, but he was an honest man, and he was fair, perhaps too fair for politics in San Francisco.

(DAN WHITE campaign speech:)
(Hear sounds of ROCKY on audio, crowd response throughout.)

DAN. Do you like my new campaign song?
(Crowd cheers.)
Yeah!

(On screen: Live video or slides of WHITE giving speech, cameras.)

DAN. *(To camera.)* For years, we have witnessed an exodus from San Francisco by many of our family members, friends and neighbors. Alarmed by the enormous increase in crime, poor educational facilities and a deteriorating social structure, they have fled to temporary havens...In a few short years these malignancies of society will erupt from our city and engulf the tree-lined, sun-bathed communities which chide us for daring to live in San Francisco. That is, unless we who have remained can transcend the apathy which has caused us to lock our doors while the tumult rages unchecked through our streets. Individually we are helpless. Yet you must realize there are thousands and thousands of angry frustrated people such as yourselves waiting to unleash a fury that can and will eradicate the malignancies which blight our beautiful city. I am not going to be forced out of San Francisco by splinter groups of radicals, social deviates, and incorrigibles. UNITE AND FIGHT WITH DAN WHITE.

(Crowd cheers.)
(Lights change.)
(Screens go to white.)

SCHMIDT. I think Dan White saw the city deteriorating as a place for the average and decent people to live.
COURT. Mr. Nothenberg, please be sworn.
SCHMIDT. The irony is...that the young man with so much promise in seeking the job on the Board of Supervisors actually was destined to construct his own downfall. After Dan White was elected he discovered there was a conflict of interest if he was a fireman and an elected official. His wife, Mary Ann, was a school teacher and made a good salary. But after their marriage, it was discovered that the wife of Dan White had become...pregnant and had to give up her teaching job. So the family income plummeted from an excess of $30,000 to $9,600 which is what a San Francisco supervisor — city councilman — is paid. I believe all the stress and the underlying mental illness culminated in his resignation that he turned in to the Mayor on November 10th, 1978.

(On screen: MR. NOTHENBERG, Deputy Mayor.)
(Lights.)

NORMAN. Would you read that for us?
NOTHENBERG. Dear Mayor Moscone: I have been proud to represent the people of San Francisco from Dis-

trict 8 for the past ten months, but due to personal responsibilities which I feel must take precedent over my legislative duties, I am resigning my position effective today. I am sure that the next representative to the Board of Supervisors will receive as much support from the people of San Francisco as I have. Sincerely, Dan White. It is so signed.

SCHMIDT. *(To jury.)* Some days after November the 10th pressure was brought to bear on Dan White to go back to the job that he had worked so hard for, and there was a one-way course that those persons could appeal to Dan White, and that was to appeal to his sense of honor: Basically — Dan you are letting the fire department down, letting the police department down. It worked. That type of pressure worked, because of the kind of man Dan White is. He asked the Mayor for his job back.

NORMAN. Mr. Nothenberg, on or about Monday the 27th of November last year, do you know whether Mayor Moscone was going to make an appointment to the Board of Supervisors, particularly for District No. 8?

NOTHENBERG. Yes, he was.

SCHMIDT. The Mayor said: We have political differences, but you are basically a good man, and you worked for the job and I'm not going to take you to fault. That letter was returned to Dan White.

NORMAN. Do you know whom his appointee to District 8 was going to be?

NOTHENBERG. Yes, I do.

NORMAN. Who was that, please.

NOTHENBERG. It was going to be a gentleman named Don Horanzey.

NORMAN. Thank you.

SCHMIDT. As I said, Dan White believed a man's word was his bond. Mayor Moscone had said: If there was any legal problem he would simply reappoint Dan White. Thereafter it became: Dan White there is no support in District 8 and unless you can show some broad base support, the job will not be given to you, and finally, the public statement coming from the Mayor's office: it's undecided. But you will be notified, prior to the time that any decision is made. They didn't tell Dan White. But they told Barbara Taylor.

(Blackout-Audio on phone.)
(Spotlight WHITE and TAYLOR.)

TAYLOR. I'm Barbara Taylor from KCBS. I'd like to speak to Dan White.
WHITE. Yuh.
TAYLOR. I have received information from a source within the Mayor's office that you are not getting that job. I am interested in doing an interview to find out your reaction to that. Mr. White?

(Long pause.)
(Spotlight DAN WHITE.)

WHITE. I don't know anything about it.

(Click.)
(Dial tone.)
(Lights change.)

TAYLOR. *(Live.)* Well, the Mayor's office told me: "The only one in favor of the appointment of Dan White is Dan White himself."

NORMAN. Thank you, Miss Taylor.

SCHMIDT. After that phone call, Denise Apcar, Dan's aide, told Dan White that there were going to be supporters down at City Hall the next morning to show support to the Mayor's office. In one day they had collected 1100 signatures in District 8 in support of Dan White.
But the next morning, Denise called Dan and told him the Mayor was unwilling to accept the petitioners.

(On screen: DENISE APCAR, Aide to DAN WHITE.)

APCAR. Yes. I told Danny — I don't remember my exact words — that the Mayor had "circumvented the people."

NORMAN. Did you believe at that time that the Mayor was going to appoint someone other than Dan White?

APCAR. Oh, yes.

NORMAN. At that time, were your feelings such that you were angry?

APCAR. Definitely. Well the Mayor had told him...and Dan always felt that a person was going to be honest when they said something. He believed that up until the end.

NORMAN. You felt and believed that Mr. Milk had been acting to prevent the appointment of Mr. Dan White to his vacated seat on the Board of Supervisors?

APCAR. Yes. I was very much aware of that.

NORMAN. Had you expressed that opinion to Mr. White?

APCAR. Yes.

NORMAN. Did Mr. White ever express that opinion also to you?

APCAR. He wasn't down at City Hall very much that week so I was basically the person that told him these things.

NORMAN. Did you call Mr. White and tell him that you had seen Harvey Milk come out of the Mayor's office after you had been informed the Mayor was not in?

APCAR. Yes, I did. Then he called me back and said, "Denise, come pick me up. I want to see the Mayor."

NORMAN. When you picked him up, did he do anything unusual?

APCAR. Well...he didn't look at me and normally he would turn his body alittle bit towards the driver and we would talk, you know, in a free-form way, but this time he didn't look at me at all. He was squinting hard. He was very nervous, he was agitated. He was rubbing his hands, blowing into his hands and rubbing them like he was cold, like his hands were cold. He acted very hurt. Yes. He was, he looked like he was going to cry. He was doing everything he could to restrain his emotion.

NORMAN. *(Looks to the jury.)* Did you ever describe him as acting quote "all fired up?" unquote.

APCAR. Yes, yes I — I believe I said that.

NORMAN. Did he mention at that time that he also was going to talk to Harvey Milk?

APCAR. Yes, he did.

NORMAN. Did he ever say he was going to quote "really lay it on the Mayor?" unquote.

APCAR. It's been brought to my attention I said

that, yes.

NORMAN. When you were driving Mr. White downtown, was there some discussion relative to a statement you made. Quote "Anger had run pretty high all week towards the Mayor playing pool on us, dirty, you know?" unquote.

APCAR. I believe I was describing my anger. At the time I made those statements I was in shock and I spoke freely and I'm sure I've never used those terms before.

NORMAN. When you made those statements it was 2 hours and 5 minutes after the killings occurred, was it not?

APCAR. Yes.

NORMAN. Miss Apcar — When you were driving Mr. White to City Hall did you know he was carrying a loaded gun?

APCAR. No. I did not.

NORMAN. Thank you.

SCHMIDT. Yes, Dan White went to City Hall and he took a .38 caliber revolver with him, and that was not particularly unusual for Dan White. Dan White was an ex-policeman, and as a policeman one is required to carry, off-duty, a gun, and as an ex-policeman — well I think it's common practice. And as it's been mentioned Dan White's life was being threatened continuously by the White Panther party and other radical groups. And additionally, remember, there was the atmosphere of terror created by the Jonestown People's Temple Tragedy.

ACT I   EXECUTION OF JUSTICE   29

(Screens flood with Jonestown image.)

Only a week before the City Hall tragedy, 900 people, mostly San Franciscans — men, women, and children — died in the jungle. Rumors surfaced that hit lists had been placed on public officials in San Francisco. Assassination squads. And in hindsight, of course, we can all realize that this did not occur, but at the time there were 900 bodies laying in Guyana to indicate that indeed people were bent on murder.

(Screen: OFFICER BYRNE, Department of Records.)
(Lights.)

NORMAN. Officer Byrne, do persons who were once on the police force who have resigned their position, do they have the right to carry a concealed firearm on their person?

SCHMIDT. And I think it will be shown that Jim Jones himself was directly allied with the liberal elements of San Francisco politics and was hostile to the conservative elements.

BYRNE. No, a resigned person would not have that right.

SCHMIDT. And so, it would be important to understand that there were threats directed towards conservative persons like Dan White.

NORMAN. Officer, have you at my instance and request examined those particular records to determine whether there is an official permit issued by the Chief of Police to a Mr. Daniel James White to carry a concealed firearm?

BYRNE. Yes, I have.
NORMAN. What have you found?
BYRNE. I find no permit.
NORMAN. Thank you.

(Lights.)

SCHMIDT. Yes, it's a violation of the law to carry a firearm without a permit, but that firearm was *registered* to Dan White. And indeed, many officials at City Hall carried guns because of this violent atmosphere including ex-police Chief, Supervisor Al Nelder and the current Mayor of San Francisco, Dianne Feinstein.
COURT. Mr. Melia, please be sworn.
SCHMIDT. Upon approaching the door on polk Street, Mr. White observed a metal detection machine.
Knowing that he did not know the man that was on the metal detection machine, he simply went around to the McAllister Street well door, where he expected to meet his aide. He did not find Denise Apcar there. She'd gone to put gas in her car. He waited for several moments, but knowing that it was imminent, the talk to the Mayor, he stepped through a window at the Department of Public Works.

(Screen: Slide of windows with man in front demonstrating procedure.)

Which doesn't require any phyical prowess, and you can step through those windows, and the evidence will show that though now they are barred, previously it was not uncommon for people to enter and exit there. They are very large windows, and are large, wide sills,

(Screen shows windows which are the windows he stepped through. They are actually small, high off the ground: Now they are barred.)

and it's quite easy to step into the building through these windows.

(On screen: Slide of man in three piece suit trying to get leg up.)
(Screen: WILLIAM MELIA JR., Civil Engineer.)

MELIA. At approximately 10:35 I heard the window open. I heard someone jump to the floor and then running through the adjoining room. I looked up and caught a glance of a man in a suit running past the doorway of my office into the City Hall hallway.

NORMAN. What did you do?

MELIA. I got up from my desk and called after him: "Hey, wait a second."

NORMAN. Did that person wait or stop?

MELIA. Yes, they did.

NORMAN. Do you see that person here in this courtroom today?

MELIA. Yes, I do.

NORMAN. Where is that person?

MELIA. It's Dan White.

(pause)

He said to me: "I had to get in. My aide was supposed to

come down and let me in the side door, but never showed up." I had taken exception to the way he had entered our office, and I replied: "AND YOU ARE?" And he replied: "I'm Dan White, the City Supervisor." He said, "Say, I've got to go," and with that, he turned and ran out of the office.

NORMAN. Did you say that he ran?

MELIA. Right.

NORMAN. Uh huh Mr. Melia — had you ever seen anyone else enter or exit through that window or those windows along that side?

MELIA. Yes, I had. It was common for individuals that worked in *our* office to do that.

NORMAN. Individuals who worked in your office...- Were you alarmed when you learned that a Supervisor crawled or walked through that window, or stepped through that window?

MELIA. Was I alarmed?

NORMAN. Yes.

MELIA. Yes. I was...alarmed.

NORMAN. Thank you.

(NORMAN looks to jury.)

SCHMIDT. *(annoyed)* I think it's significant at this point — also because the fact that he crawled through the window *appears* to be important — it's significant to re-iterate that as Mr. Melia just testified people *often climb through that window,* and indeed, on the morning of the 27th, Denise had the key to the McAllister Street well door. *So,* Dan White stepped through the window, identified

ACT I EXECUTION OF JUSTICE 33

himself, traveled up to the second floor.

(Screen: MRS. CYR COPERTINI, appointment secretary to the Mayor.)

And then approached the desk of Cyr Copertini and properly identified himself, and asked to see the Mayor.

(Lights.)

CYR. I am the appointment secretary to Mayor Feinstein.
NORMAN. In November of last year and particularly on November 27th what was your then occupation?
CYR. I was appointment secretary to the Elected Mayor of San Francisco, George Moscone.

(WITNESS deeply moved.)

NORMAN. Mrs. Copertini — Were you aware that there was anything that was going to happen that day of November 27th of interest to the citizens of San Francisco, uh...I mean, such as some public announcement?
CYR. ...There was to be a news conference to announce the new supervisor for the Eighth District, at 11:30.
NORMAN. Mrs. Copertini, at approximately 10:30 a.m. you saw Mr. Daniel White, he appeared in front of your desk...do you recall what he said?
CYR. He said: "Hello, Cyr. May I see the Mayor?" I said: "He has someone with him, but let me go check

with him.." I went into the Mayor and told him that Supervisor White was there to see him. He was a little dismayed. He was a little uncomfortable by it and said: "Oh, all right. Tell him I'll see him, but he will have to wait a coupla minutes."
I asked the Mayor, "Shouldn't I have someone in there with him," and he said: "No, no, I'll see him alone."
And I asked him again. And he said,
"No, no, I'll see him alone." And then I went back.
I said to Dan White, "it will be a few minutes."
He asked me how I was and how things were going. Was I having a nice day.

NORMAN. Was there anything unusual about his tone of voice?

CYR. No. I don't think so. He seemed nervous.
I asked him would he like to see the newspaper while he was waiting? He said: "No, he wouldn't," and I said: "Well, that's all right. There's nothing in it anyway unless you want to read about Caroline Kennedy having turned 21." And he said: "21? Is that right." He said: "Yeah, that's all so long ago. It's even more amazing when you think that John John is now 18."

(Lights change. Music "Deus Irae")
(Boy's Choir.)

DENMAN. The only comparable situation I ever remember was when JFK was killed.

CYR. It was about that time he was admitted to the Mayor's office.

NORMAN. Did you tell Mr. Daniel White that he could

go in?
CYR. Yes.
DENMAN. I remember that in my bones, in my body.
NORMAN. Did he respond in any way to that?
DENMAN. Just like this one.
CYR. He said: "Good girl, Cyr."
NORMAN. Good girl, Cyr?
CYR. Right.
DENMAN. when Camelot all of a sudden turned to hell.
NORMAN. Then what did he do?
CYR. Went in.
NORMAN. After he went in there did you hear anything of an unusual nature that was coming from the Mayor's office?
CYR. After a time I heard a...commotion.

(Lights change.)

YOUNG MOTHER. I heard it on the car radio, I literally gasped.
NORMAN. Explain that to us, please.
YOUNG MOTHER. I wanted to pull over to the side of the road and scream.
CYR. Well, I heard — a series of noises — first a group and then one—
YOUNG MOTHER. Just scream.
CYR. I went to the window to see if anything was happening out in the street.
YOUNG MOTHER. Then I thought of my kids.

CYR. and the street was rather extraordinarily calm.

DENMAN. I noticed when I looked outside that there was an unusual quiet.

CYR. For that hour of the day there is usually more — there wasn't really anything out there.

DENMAN. I went to the second floor and started walking toward the Mayor's office.

YOUNG MOTHER. I wanted to get them out of school and take them home,

NORMAN. Could you describe these noises for us?

YOUNG MOTHER. I wanted to take them home and *(SHE makes a hugging gesture with her arms.)* lock the door.

CYR. Well, they were dull thuds rather like—

DENMAN. And there was this strange combination of panic and silence that you rarely see,

CYR. I thought maybe it was an automobile door that somebody had tried to shut, by, you know, pushing, and then finally succeeding.

DENMAN. It was like a silent slow-motion movie of a disaster.

NORMAN. Do you have any recollection that you can report with any certainty to us as to how many sounds there were?

CYR. No. As I stood there I — I thought I ought to remember— *(WITNESS breaks down.)*

DENMAN. There was this hush and aura, people were moving with strange faces, as if the world had just come to an end.

NOTHENBERG. *(MOSCONE's friend.)* George loved this city, and felt what was wrong could be fixed.

NORMAN. Do you want a glass of water?

(CYR sobs.)

DENMAN. And I asked someone what had happened and he said: "The Mayor has been shot."
CYR. I ought to remember that pattern in case it is something, but I—
NOTHENBERG. *(MOSCONE's friend.)* He knew — it was a white racist town. A Catholic town. But he believed in people's basic good will.

(CYR sobs.)

COURT. Just a minute. Do you want a recess?
NOTHENBERG. *(MOSCONE's friend.)* He never suspected, I bet, Dan White's psychotic behavior.
NORMAN. Do you want a recess?
NOTHENBERG. *(MOSCONE's friend.)* That son of a bitch killed someone I loved. I mean, I loved the guy.
CYR. No. I'm all right.
COURT. Are you sure you are all right?
CYR. Yes.
YOUNG MOTHER. I just thought of my kids.

(pause)

NOTHENBERG. *(MOSCONE's friend.)* I loved his idealism. I loved his hope.
CYR. Then what happened was Rudy Nothenberg left to tell the press that the conference would start a few

minutes late.

NOTHENBERG. *(MOSCONE's friend.)* I loved the guy.

CYR. And then he came back to me right away and said: "Oh, I guess we can go ahead. I just saw Dan White leave."

NOTHENBERG. *(MOSCONE's friend.)* I loved his almost naive faith in people.

CYR. So then he went into the Mayor's office and said: "Well, he's not here." And I said: "Well, maybe he went into the back room."

NOTHENBERG. *(MOSCONE's friend.)* I loved his ability to go on.

CYR. Then he just gave a shout saying: "Gary, get in here. Call an ambulance. Get the police."

NOTHENBERG. See, I got too tired to stay in politics and do it. George and I were together from the beginning. Me, Phil Burton, Willie Brown. Beatin' all the old Irishmen.

DENMAN. I heard right away that Dan White had done it.

NOTHENBERG. But George believed, as corny as this sounds, that you do good for the people. I haven't met many of those and George was one of those. Maybe those are the guys that get killed. I don't know.

(CYR crying.)

NORMAN. All right. All this you told us about occurred in San Francisco, didn't it?

CYR. *(Deeply moved.)* Yes.

SCHMIDT. Dan White, as it was quite apparent at that

point had CRACKED because of his underlying mental illness...

(Screen: CARL HENRY CARLSON, Aide to HARVEY MILK.)

CARLSON. I heard Peter Nardoza, Diane Feinstein's aide, say: Diane wants to see you and Dan White said: "That'll have to wait a couple of minutes, I have something to do first."
NORMAN. I have something to do first?
CARLSON. Yes.
NORMAN. Do you recall in what manner Mr. White announced himself?
SCHMIDT. There were stress factors due to the fact that he hadn't been notified,
CARLSON. He appeared at the door which was normally left open. Stuck his head in and asked: "Say, Harv, can I see you for a minute?"
SCHMIDT. and the sudden emotional surge that he had in the Mayor's office was simply too much for him
NORMAN. What did Harvey Milk do at that time if anything?
CARLSON. He turned around.
SCHMIDT. and he cracked.
CARLSON. He turned around
SCHMIDT. The man cracked.
CARLSON. and said "Sure." and got up and went across the hall...
SCHMIDT. He shot the Mayor,
CARLSON. to the office designated as Dan White's office on the chart.

SCHMIDT. reloaded his gun, basically on *instinct*, because of his police training, and was about to leave the building at that point

NORMAN. After they went across the hall to Mr. White's office...

SCHMIDT. and he looked down the hall,

NORMAN. Would you tell us what next you heard or saw?

SCHMIDT. he saw somebody that he believed to be an aide to Harvey Milk.

CARLSON. A few seconds, probably 10, 15 seconds later, I heard a shot, or the sound of gunfire.

SCHMIDT. He went down to the Supervisor's area to *talk* to Harvey Milk.

COURT. Excuse me. Would you speak out. Your voice is fading a bit.

SCHMIDT. At that point, in the same state of rage, emotional upheaval with the stress of 10 years of mental illness having cracked this man.

CORONER. *(Demonstrates as HE speaks.)* The left arm has to be close to the body and slightly forward with the palm up.

SCHMIDT. *ninety seconds* from the time he shot the Mayor, Dan White shot and killed Harvey Milk.

CARLSON. After the shot, I heard Harvey Milk scream. "oh, no." And then the first — the first part of the second "no" which was then cut short by the second shot.

CORONER. The right hand has to be palm away with the thumb pointed towards the body and the elbow in slightly to the body with the arm raised.

NORMAN. How many sounds of shots did you hear

altogether, Mr. Carlson?

CARLSON. Five or six. I really didn't consciously count them.

CORONER. In this position all of these wounds that I have just described in Peoples's 30 and 29 line up.

(Blackout on CORONER in position.)
(Pause.)

CARLSON. A few moments later the door opened, the door opened, and Daniel White walked out, rushed out, and proceeded down the hall.

NORMAN. Now, Mr. Carlson, when Daniel White first appeared at the office of Harvey Milk and said, "Say, Harv, can I see you for a minute?", could you describe his tone of voice in any way?

CARLSON. He appeared to be very normal, usual friendly self. I didn't, I didn't feel anything out of the ordinary. It was just very typical Dan White.

(Music out, lights change.)

GWENN. I'd like to talk about when people are pushed to the wall.

SCHMIDT. Harvey Milk was against the re-appointment of Dan White.

GWENN. In order to understand the riots, I think you have to understand that the Dan White verdict did not occur in a vacuum.

SCHMIDT. Basically, it was a political decision. It was evident there was a liberal wing of the Board of Supervisors, and there was a smaller conservative wing, and Dan White was a conservative politician for San Francisco.

(Screen: RICHARD PABICH, Legislative Assistant to HARVEY MILK.)
(Lights.)

PABICH. My address is 542-A Castro Street.

GWENN. I don't think I have to say what their presence meant to us, and what their loss meant to us—

NORMAN. What did you do after you saw Dan White run down the hall and put the key in the door of his old office, Room 237?

GWENN. The assassinations of our friends Harvey Milk and George Moscone were a crime against us all.

PABICH. Well, I was struck in my head, sort of curious as to why he'd been running.

GWENN. And right here, when I say "us," I don't mean only gay people.

PABICH. And he was — it looked like he was in a hurry. I was aware of the political situation.

GWENN. I mean all people who are getting less than they deserve.

PABICH. I was aware that Harvey was taking the position to the Mayor that Mr. White shouldn't be reappointed. Harvey and I had talked earlier that day...that it would be a significant day.

(Lights.)
(Subliminal music.)

MILK'S FRIEND. After Harvey died, I went into a depression that lasted about a year, I guess. They called it depression, anyway. I thought about suicide, well, I more than thought about it.

SCHMIDT. Mr. Pabich, Mr. Milk had suggested a replacement for Dan White, hadn't he?

PABICH. He had, to my understanding, recommended several people, and basically took the position that Dan White should not be reappointed.

MILK'S FRIEND. I lost my job. I stayed in the hospital for, I would guess, two months or so. They put me on some kind of drug that...well, it helped, I guess. I mean, I loved him and it was...

SCHMIDT. Was he requesting that a homosexual be appointed?

PABICH. No, he was not.

MILK'S FRIEND. Well, he was gone and that couldn't change.

SCHMIDT. I have nothing further. Thank you.

MILK'S FRIEND. He'd never be here again, I knew that.

COURT. All right. Any redirect, Mr. Norman?

NORMAN. No. Thank you for coming, Mr. Pabich. *(PABICH exits.)*

GWENN. It was as if Dan White had given the go-ahead. It was a free-for-all, a license to kill.

(PABICH with JOANNA LU.)
(TV lights.)

PABICH. *(On camera.)* It's over. Already I can tell it's

over. He asked me a question, a clear queer-baiting question, and the jury didn't bat an eye. *(Starts to exit, then.)* Dan White's going to get away with murder.

JOANNA LU. Mr. Pabich.

MILK'S FRIEND. I had this recurring dream. We were at the Opera, Harvey and I. I was laughing. Harvey was laughing. Then Harvey leaned over and said to me: When you're watching Tosca, you know you're alive. That's when I'd wake up.

GWENN. I remember the moment I heard Harvey had been shot— *(SHE breaks down.)*

MILK'S FRIEND. And I'd realize — like for the first time all over again — he's dead.

(Blackout.)

(Hyperreal sounds of high heels on marble, echoing, moving fast. Mumbled Hail Marys.)
(Fade lights up slowly on SCHMIDT, NORMAN.)

SCHMIDT. From here I think the evidence will demonstrate that Dan White ran down to Denise's office, screamed at his aide to give him the key to her car. And he left, went to a church, called his wife, went into St. Mary's Cathedral, prayed, and his wife got there, and he told her, the best he could, what he remembered he had done, and then they walked together to the Northern Police Station where he turned himself in; asked the officer to look after his wife, asked the officer to take possession of an Irish poster he was carrying...

(Screen: Slide: Stain glass window, cover of Uris book.)
(IRELAND: A Terrible Beauty.)

and then made a statement, what best he could recall had occurred. *(FALZON hands on shoulders.)*

FALZON. Why...I feel like hitting you in the fuckin' mouth...How could you be so stupid? How?

WHITE. I...I want to tell you about it...I want to, to explain.

FALZON. Do you want a lawyer, Danny?

WHITE. No, Frank I want to talk to you.

FALZON. Okay, if you want to talk to me, I'm gonna get my tape recorder and read you your rights and do it right.

NORMAN. The people at this time move the tape recorded statement into evidence.

FALZON. Today's date is Monday, November 27th, 1978. The time is presently 12:05. We're inside the Homicide Detail, Room 454, at the Hall of Justice. Present is Inspector Edward Erdelatz, Inspector Frank Falzon and for the record, sir, your full name?

WHITE. Daniel James White.

FALZON. Would you, normally in a situation like this, ah...we ask questions, I'm aware of your past history as a police officer and also as a San Francisco fireman. I would prefer, I'll let you do it in a narrative form as to what happened this morning if you can lead up to the events of the shooting and then backtrack as to why these events took place. *(Looks at ERDELATZ.)*

WHITE. Well, it's just that I've been under an awful lot of pressure lately, financial pressure, because of my job situation, family pressure because of ah...not being able to have the time with my family. *(sob)*

FALZON. Can you relate these pressures you've been under, Dan, at this time? Can you explain it to Inspector Erdelatz and myself.

WHITE. It's just that I wanted to serve *(FALZON nods.)* the people of San Francisco well and I did that. Then when the pressures got too great, I decided to leave. After I left, my family and friends offered their support and said, whatever it would take to allow me to go back into office, — well, they would be willing to make that effort. And then it came out that Supervisor Milk and some others were working against me to get my seat back on the Board. He didn't speak to me, he spoke to the City Attorney but I was in the office and I heard the conversation.

I could see the game that was being played, they were going to use me as a *scapegoat,* whether I was a good supervisor or not, was not the point. This was a political opportunity and they were going to degrade me and my family and the job that I had tried to do an, an more or less HANG ME OUT TO DRY. And I saw more and more evidence of this during the week when the papers reported that ah...someone else was going to be reappointed. The Mayor told me he was going to call me before he made any decision, he never did that. I was troubled, the pressure, my family again, my, my son's out to a babysitter.

FALZON. Dan, can you tell Inspector Erdelatz and myself, what was your plan this morning? What did you have in mind?

WHITE. I didn't have any devised plan or anything, it's, I was leaving the house to talk, to see the Mayor and I went downstairs, to, to make a phone call and I had my gun down there.

FALZON. Is this your police service revolver, Dan?

WHITE. This is the gun I had when I was a policeman. It's in my room an ah...I don't know, I just put it on. I, I don't know why I put it on, it's just...

FALZON. You went directly from your residence to the Mayor's office this morning?

WHITE. Yes, my, my aide picked me up but she didn't have any idea ah...you know that I had a gun on me or, you know, and I went in to see him an, an he told me he wasn't going to reappoint me and he wasn't intending to tell me about it. Then ah...I got kind of fuzzy and then just my head didn't feel right and I,

FALZON. Was this before any threats on your part, Dan?

WHITE. I, I never made any threats.

FALZON. There were no threats at all?

WHITE. I, I...oh no.

FALZON. When were you, how, what was the conversation, can you explain to Inspector Erdelatz and myself the conversation that existed between the two of you at this time?

WHITE. It was pretty much just, you know, I asked, was I going to be reappointed. He said, no I am not, no you're not. And I said, why, and he told me, it's a political decision and that's the end of it, and that's it and then he could obviously see, see I was obviously distraught an then he said, let's have a drink and I, I'm not even a drinker, you know I don't, once in a while, but I'm not even a drinker. But I just kinda stumbled in the back and he was all, he was all smiles — he was talking an nothing was getting through to me. It was just like a roaring in my ears an, an then...it just came to me, you know, he...

FALZON. You couldn't hear what he was saying, Dan?

WHITE. Just small talk that, you know, it just wasn't registering. What I was going to do now, you know, and how this would affect my family, you know, an, an just, just all the time knowing he's going to go out an, an lie to the press an, an tell 'em, you know, that I, I wasn't a good supervisor and that people didn't want me an then that was it. Then I, I just shot him, that was it, it was over.

FALZON. What happened after you left there, Dan?

WHITE. Well, I, I left his office by one of the back doors an, I was going to go down the stairs and then I saw Harvey Milk's aide across the hall at the Supervisor's an then it struck me about what Harvey had tried to do an I said, well I'll go talk to him. He didn't know I had, I had heard his conversation and he was all smiles and stuff and I went in and, you know, I, I didn't agree with him on a lot of things but I was always honest, you know, and here they were devious. And then he started kinda smirking, 'cause he knew, he knew I wasn't going to be reappointed. And ah...I started to say you know how hard I worked for it and what it meant to me and my family and then my reputation as, as a hard worker, good honest person and he just kind of smirked at me as if to say, too bad an then, and then, I just got all flushed an, an hot, and I shot him.

FALZON. This occurred inside your roon, Dan?

WHITE. Yeah, in my office, yeah.

ACT I   EXECUTION OF JUSTICE   49

FALZON. And when you left there did you go back home?

WHITE. No, no, no I drove to the, the Doggie Diner on, on Van Ness and I called my wife and she, she didn't know, she...

FALZON. Did you tell her, Dan?

(Sobbing.)

WHITE. I called up, I didn't tell her on the phone. I just said ... she was working. I just told her to meet me at the cathedral.

FALZON. St. Mary's?

(Sobbing.)

WHITE. She took a cab, yeah. She didn't know. She knew I'd been upset and I wasn't even talking to her at home because I just couldn't explain how I felt and she had no, nothing to blame about it, she was, she always has been great to me but it was, just the pressure hitting me an just my head's all flushed and expected that my skull's going to crack. Then when she came to the church, I, I told her and she kind of slumped an she, she couldn't say anything.

FALZON. How is she now do you, do you know is she, do you know where she is?

WHITE. I don't know now. She, she came to Northern Station with me. She asked me not to do anything about myself, you know that she, she loved me and she'd stick by me and not to hurt myself.

ERDELATZ. Dan, right now are you under a doctor's care?
WHITE. No.
ERDELATZ. Are you under any medication at all?
WHITE. No.
ERDELATZ. When is the last time you had your gun with you prior to today?
WHITE. I guess it was a few months ago. I, I was afraid of some of the threats that were made an, I, I, just wanted to make sure to protect myself you know this, this city isn't safe you know and there's a lot of people running around an well I don't have to tell you fellows, you guys know that.
ERDELATZ. When you left home this morning, Dan, was it your intention to confront the Mayor, Supervisor Milk or anyone else with that gun?
WHITE. No, I, I, what I wanted to do was just, talk to him, you know, I, I ah, I didn't even know if I was going to be reappointed or not be reappointed. *Why do we do things, you know, why did I, I don't know. No, I,* I just wanted to talk to him that's all an at least have him be honest with me and tell me why he was doing it, not because I was a bad supervisor or anything but, you know, I never killed anybody before, I never shot anybody...
ERDELATZ. Why did...
WHITE. ....I didn't even, I didn't even know if I wanted to kill him. I just shot him, I don't know.
ERDELATZ. What type of gun is that you were carrying, Dan?
WHITE. It's a .38, a two-inch .38.
ERDELATZ. And do you know how many shots you

fired?

WHITE. Uh...no I don't, I don't. I, I out of instinct when I, I reloaded the gun ah...you know, it's just the training I guess I had, you know.

ERDELATZ. Where did you reload?

WHITE. I reloaded in my office, when I was I couldn't out in the hall.

(Pause.)

ERDELATZ. When you say you reloaded, are you speaking of following the shooting in the Mayor's office?

WHITE. Yeah.

ERDELATZ. Inspector Falzon?

FALZON. No questions. Is there anything you'd like to add, Dan, before we close this statement?

WHITE. Yes. Just that I've been honest and worked hard, never cheated anybody and I wanted to do a good job, I'm trying to do a good job and I saw this city as it's going, kind of downhill and I was always just a lonely vote on the board. I was trying to do a good job for the city.

FALZON. Inspector Erdelatz and I ah...appreciate your cooperation and the truthfulness of your statement.

(Lights change.)
(DAN WHITE sobbing. MARY ANNE WHITE sobbing, JURORS sobbing.)
(FALZON moved.)

NORMAN. I think that is all. You may examine.

COURT. Do you want to take a recess at this time?
SCHMIDT. Why don't we take a brief recess?
COURT. Let me admonish you, ladies and gentlemen of the jury, not to discuss this case among yourselves nor with anyone else, not allow anyone to speak to you about the matter, no are you to form or express an opinion until the matter has been submitted to you.

(Gavel.)
(House light up.)
(On screen: Recess.)

INTERMISSION

ACT II

IN DEFENSE OF MURDER

*AS AUDIENCE ENTERS, ON SCREEN
DOCUMENTARY IMAGES OF MILK AND MOSCONE
COMPANY/AUDIENCE WATCH*

MOSCONE. * My late father was a guard at San Quentin, and who I was visiting one day, and who showed to me, and then explained the function of, the uh, the uh death chamber. And it just seemed inconceivable to me, though I was pretty young at the time, that in this society that I had been trained to believe was the most effective and efficient of all societies, that the only way we could deal with violent crime would be to do the ultimate ourselves, and that's to governmentally sanction the taking of another person's life.

MILK. * *(FALZON enters.)* Two days after I was elected I got a phone call — the voice was quite young. It was from Altoona, Pennsylvania. And the person said, "Thanks." And you've got to elect gay people so that that young child, and the thousands upon thousands like that child,

---

*Dialogue from *The Times of Harvey Milk*, a film by Robert Epstein and Richard Schmeichen.

* know that there's hope for a better world. There's hope for a better tomorrow. Without hope, they'll only gaze at those blacks, the Asians, the disabled, the seniors, the us'es, the us'es. Without hope, the us'es give up. I know that you cannot live on hope alone. But without it, life is not worth living. And you, and you, and you, gotta give 'em hope. Thank you very much.

(Lights up. Courtroom.)
(FALZON on witness stand.)
(DAN WHITE at defense table sobbing.)
(MARY ANN WHITE behind him sobbing.)
(On tape.)

WHITE. *(voice)* Just that I've been honest and worked hard, never cheated anybody and I wanted to do a good job, I'm trying to do a good job and I saw this city as it's going, kind of downhill and I was always just a lonely vote on the board. I was trying to do a good job for the city.

FALZON. Inspector Erdelatz and I ah...
appreciate your cooperation and the truthfulness of your statement.

(FALZON SWITCHES TAPE OFF.)

NORMAN. I think that is all. You may examine.
(Lights change, company exits.)

---

*Dialogue from *The Times of Harvey Milk*, a film by Robert Epstein and Richard Schmeichen.

(On screen: INSPECTOR FRANK FALZON, witness for the prosecution.)
(Dissolve to on screen: ACT TWO — IN DEFENSE OF MURDER.)

SCHMIDT. Inspector Falzon, you mentioned that you had known Dan White in the past, prior to November 27, 1978?

FALZON. Yes, sir, quite well.

SCHMIDT. About how long have you known him?

FALZON. According to Dan,
it goes way back to the days
we attended St. Elizabeth's Grammar School together,
but we went to different high schools.
I attended St. Ignatius, and he attended Riordan.
He walked up to me one day at the Jackson Playground,
with spikes over his shoulders, glove in his hand,
and asked if he could play on the team.
I told him it was the police team,
and he stated that he was a new recruit at Northern Station,
wanted to play on the police softball team,
and since that day Dan White and I
have been very good friends.

SCHMIDT. You knew him fairly well then, that is fair?

FALZON. As well as I know anybody, I believed.

SCHMIDT. Can you tell me, when you saw him first on November 27th, 1978, how did he appear physically to you?

FALZON. Destroyed. This was not the Dan White I had

known, not at all.
That day I saw a shattered individual,
both mentally and physically in apearance,
who appeared to me to be shattered.
Dan White, the man I knew
prior to Monday, the 27th of November, 1978,
was a man among men.

SCHMIDT. Knowing, with regard to the shootings of Mayor Moscone and Harvey Milk, knowing Dan White as you did, is he the type of man that could have premeditatedly and deliberately shot those people?

NORMAN. Objection as calling for an opinion and conclusion.

COURT. Sustained.

SCHMIDT. Knowing him as you do, have you ever seen anything in his past that would lead you to believe he was capable of cold-bloodedly shooting somebody?

NORMAN. Same objection.

COURT. Sustained.

SCHMIDT. Your Honor, at this point I have anticipated that maybe there would be some argument with regard to opinions not only as to Inspector Falzon, but with a number of other witnesses that I intend to call, and accordingly I have prepared a memorandum of what I believe to be the appropriate law. *(Shows memo.)*

COURT. I have no quarrel with your authorities, but I think the form of the questions that you asked was objectionable.

SCHMIDT. The questions were calculated to bring out an opinion on the state of mind and — I believe that a lay person, if he is an intimate acquaintance, surely can hazard such an opinion. I believe that Inspector Falzon, as a police officer, has an opinion.

COURT. Get the facts from this witness. I will let you get those facts, whatever they are.

SCHMIDT. All right, we will try that.
Inspector Falzon, again, you mentioned that you were quite familiar with Dan White; can you tell me something about the man's character, as to the man that you knew prior to the — prior to November 27th, 1978?

NORMAN. Objection as being irrelevant and vague.

COURT. Overruled. *(To FALZON.)* Do you understand the question?

FALZON. I do, basically, your Honor.

COURT. All right, you may answer it.

NORMAN. Well, your Honor, character for what?

COURT. Overruled. *(To FALZON.)* You may answer it.

FALZON. The Dan White that I knew prior to Monday, November 27, 1978, was a man who seemed to excel in pressure situations,

and it seemed that the greater the pressure, the more enjoyment

that Dan had,

exceeding at what he was trying to do.

Examples would be in his sports life,

that I can relate to,

and for the first time in the history of the State of California,

there was a law enforcement softball tournament held in 1971.

The San Francisco Police Department entered
that softball tournament along with other major departments,
Los Angeles included,
and Dan White was not only named on the All Star Team
at the end of the tournament,
but named the most valuable player.

He was just outstanding under pressure situations,
when men would be on base
and that clutch hit was needed.

Another example of Dan White's
attitude toward pressure
was that when he decided to run
for the District 8 Supervisor's seat,
and I can still vividly remember the morning
he walked into the Homicide Detail and sat down to—
announce that he was going to run for City Supervisor,

I said: "How are you going to do it, Dan?
Nobody heard of Dan White.
How are you going to go out there,
win this election?

He said: "I'm going to do it the way the people
want it to be done,

knock on their doors, go inside, shake their hands,
let them know what Dan White stands for."

And he said: "Dan White is going to represent them.
There will be a voice in City Hall, you watch, I'll
make it."

He did what he said he was going to do,
he ran, won the election.

SCHMIDT. Given these things that you mentioned about Dan White, outstanding under pressure, there anything in his character that you saw of him, prior to those tragedies of the 27th of November, that would have led you to believe that he would ever kill somebody cold-bloodedly?

NORMAN. Objection, irrelevant.

COURT. Overruled.

NORMAN. Let me state my grounds for the record.

COURT. Overruled.

NORMAN. Thank you, Judge.

It's irrelevant and called for his opinion and speculation.

COURT. Overruled. *(Gavel. To FALZON.)* You may answer that.

FALZON. Yes, your Honor.

I'm aware — I'm hesitating only because
there was something I saw in Dan's personality
that didn't become relevant to me
until I was assigned this case.
He had a tendency to run, occasionally,
from situations.

I saw this flaw, and I asked him about it,
and his response was that his ultimate goal
was to purchase a boat, just travel around the world,
get away from everybody,

He wanted to be helpful to people,
and yet he wanted to run away from them.
That did not make sense to me.

Otherwise, to me,
Dan White was an exemplary indiviual,
a man that I was proud to know
and be associated with.

SCHMIDT. Do you think he cracked? Do you think there was something wrong with him on November 27th?

NORMAN. Objection as calling for an opinion and speculation.

COURT. Sustained.

SCHMIDT. I have nothing further. *(Turns back.)* Inspector, I have one last question. Did you ever see him act out of revenge as to the whole time you have known him?

NORMAN. Objection. That calls for speculation.

COURT. No, overruled, and this is as to his observations and contacts. Overruled.

FALZON. The only time Dan White
could have acted out in revenge
is when he took the opposite procedure
in hurting himself,

by quitting the San Francisco Police Department.

SCHMIDT. Nothing further. Thank you, sir.

NORMAN. Inspector Falzon, you regard yourself as a close friend to Mr. Daniel White, don't you?

FALZON. Yes, sir.

NORMAN. Do you regard yourself as a *very* close friend of Mr. Daniel Whtie.

FALZON. I would consider myself a close friend of yours, if that can relate to you my closeness with Dan White.

NORMAN. Of course, you haven't known me as long as you have known Mr. Daniel White, have you, Inspector?

FALZON. Just about the same length of time, Counsel.

NORMAN. Inspector Falzon, while you've expressed some shock at these tragedies, would you subscribe to the proposition that there's a first for everything?

FALZON. It's obvious in this case; yes, sir.

NORMAN. Thank you.

(NORMAN sits.)
(FALZON gets up and takes his seat.)
(Beside NORMAN.)

NORMAN. The Prosecution rests.

(Blackout.)

(On screen: The Prosecution rests.)
(Commotion in court.)

COURT. Order.

(Gavel.)
(Lights up.)
(FREITAS alone.)

FREITAS. I was the D.A.
Obviously in some respects, the trial ruined me. This trial...

(On screen: Dissolve into picture of DAN WHITE as fire hero.)
(Screen: THE DEFENSE. Subliminal music.)
(Lights up.)

SHERRATT. *(Fire Chief)* Dan White was an exellent fire fighter. In fact, he was commended for a rescue at Geneva Towers. The award hasn't been given to him as yet, uh...

FREDIANI. *(Fireman)* Dan White was the valedictorian of the Fire Department class. He was voted so by members of the class.

(On screen: DAN WHITE as Valedictorian.)

MILK'S FRIEND. When I was in the hospital, what galled me most was the picture of Dan White as the ALL American Boy.

SHERRATT. but a meritorious advisory board and fire commission were going to present Mr. White with a class C medal.

(On screen: DAN WHITE as fire hero.)

FREDIANI. Everybody liked Dan.
SCHMIDT. Did you work with Dan as a policeman?
SULLIVAN. *(Policeman)* Yes, I did.
MILK'S FRIEND. Maybe as a gay man, I understand the tyranny of the All American Boy.

(On screen: DAN WHITE as police officer.)

FREDIANI. He loved sports and I loved sports.

(On screen: DAN WHITE as golden gloves boxer.)

SULLIVAN. Dan White as a police officer,
was a very fair police officer on the street.
MILK'S FRIEND. Maybe because I am so often his victim.
GWENN. I followed the trial in the papers.
SCHMIDT. Having had the experience of being a police officer, is it unusual for persons that have been police officers to carry guns?
SULLIVAN. Uh, pardon me, Mr. Schmidt?
GWENN. I thought then something was wrong with this picture.
SCHMIDT. I say, it is uncommon that ex-police officers would carry guns?
GWENN. Something was wrong, we thought, when the Chief Inspector of Homicide became the chief character witness for the defense.
SULLIVAN. No, it is a common thing that former police

officers will carry guns.

GWENN. Why didn't the Chief Inspector of Homicide ask Dan White how he got into City Hall with a loaded gun?

SCHMIDT. With out a permit?

SULLIVAN. Yes.

GWENN. Dan White reloaded after shooting the Mayor. If it was "reflex," police training, why didn't he reload again after shooting Harvey Milk?

SCHMIDT. Is there anything in his character that would have led you to believe he was capable of shooting two persons?

NORMAN. Objection.

COURT. Overruled.

SULLIVAN. No, nothing whatever.

GWENN. And what can explain the coup de grace shots
White fired into the backs of their heads as they lay there helpless on the floor?

DOLSON. *(City Supervisor)* Dan in my opinion was a person who saved lives.

GWENN. Where is the prosecution?

FREITAS. I mean, I would have remained in politics. Except for this. I was voted out of office.

SCHMIDT. *(To DOLSON.)* Supervisor Dolson, you saw him on
November 27th, 1978, did you not?

DOLSON. I did.

FREITAS. In hindsight, you know.
I would have changed a lot of things.

SCHMIDT. What did you see?

FREITAS. But hindsight is always perfect vision.

(Slide: DAN WHITE as City Supervisor outside City Hall.)

DOLSON. What I saw made me want to cry...
Dan was always so neat.
Looked like a Marine on Parade...
  GWENN. What pressures were you under *indeed?*
  DOLSON. And here he was, this kid, who was badly disheveled
and he had his hands cuffed behind him,
which was something I never expected to see.
He looked *(sobs)* absolutely *devastated.*
  GWENN. As the "VICTIM" sat in the courtroom
we heard of policemen and firemen sporting
FREE DAN WHITE t-shirts
as they raised 100,000 dollars for Dan White's defense fund,
and the same message began appearing
in spray paint on walls around the city.
FREE DAN WHITE.
  DOLSON. I put my arm around him, told him that everything
was going to be all right,
but how everything was going to be all right,
I don't know.

(WITNESS deeply moved)
(MARY ANN WHITE sobs.)

GWENN. And the trial was still happening.
SCHMIDT. *(Deeply moved.)* Thank you. I have nothing further.

(DOLSON sobs.)

GWENN. but the tears at the Hall of Justice are all for Dan White.

(Gavel.)
(They exit.)
(Lights change.)

(The ex-D.A. alone in an empty courtroom.)
(Nervous, fidgeting.)

FREITAS. I was voted out of office.

(On screen: JOSEPH FREITAS, JR., former D.A.)

Well, I'm out of politics and I don't know whether
I'll get back into politics
because it certainly did set back my personal ah...
aspirations as a public figure dramatically.
I don't know.

You know, there was an attempt to not allow our office to
prosecute the case
because I was close to Moscone myself.
And we fought against that.

I was confident—
(laughs)
I chose Tom Norman because he was the senior homicide prosecutor
for fifteen years and he was quite successful at it.
I don't know...

The was a great division in the city then, you know.
The city was divided all during that period.
George was a liberal Democrat and Dick Hongisto.
I was considered a lilberal Democrat
and George as you'll remember was elected
Mayor over John Barbagelata who was the leader
of what was considered the Right in town.
And it was a narrow victory.
So, after his election, Barbagelata persisted in attacking them
and keeping
I thought—
keeping the city divided.

It divided on emerging constituencies like
the gay constituency.
That's the one that was used to cause
the most divisive emotions more than any other.
So the divisiveness in the city was there.

I mean that was the whole point of this political fight
between Dan White
and Moscone and Milk:

The fight was over who controlled the city.

The Right couldn't afford to lose Dan.
He was their Saving vote on the Board of Supervisors.
He blocked the Milk/Moscone agenda.
Obviously Harvey Milk didn't want Dan White on the Board.

So, it was political, the murders.

Maybe I should have,
again in hindsight, possible Tom,
even though his attempts to do that may have been ruled inadmissible,
possible Tom should have been a little stronger in that area.
But again, at the time...I mean,
even the press was shocked at the outcome...

But—
Well, I think that what the jury had already bought was
White's background—
Now that's what was really on trial.
Dan White sat there and waved his little American flag
and they acquitted him.
They convicted George and Harvey.
Now if this had been a poor Black or a poor Chicano
or a poor white janitor who'd been fired,
or the husband of an alleged girlfriend of Moscone's

I don't think they would have bought the diminished capacity
defense.
But whereas they have a guy who was a member of a
county Board of Supervisors who left the police department,
who had served in the army, who was a fireman,
who played baseball—
I think that's what they were caught up in —
that kind of person *must* have been crazy to do this.
I would have interpreted it differently.
Not to be held to a higher standard, but uh...
that he had all the tools to be responsible.

One of the things people said was:
"Why didn't you talk more about
George's background, his family life, etc.?"
Well...
One of the reasons is that Tom Norman did know,
that had he opened up that area,

they were prepared,
yeah—
they were prepared to smear George—to bring up the incident in
Sacramento. With the Woman—
(And other things.)
It would be at best a wash,
so why get into it?

If you know they're going to bring out things that aren't positive.
We wanted to let the city heal.
We — And after Jonestown...
Well it would have been the city on trial.
If the jury had stuck to the facts alone,
I mean, the confession alone was enough to convict him...
I mean, look at this kid that shot Reagan,
it was the same thing. All they way through that,
they said, my friends—
"Well, Christ, look at what the prosecutors went through on that one, Joe.
It's tragic that that has to be the kind of experience
that will make you feel better.

And then about White being anti-gay
well...
White inside himself may have been anti-gay, but
that Milk was his target...
As I say — *Malice was there.*
Milk led the fight to keep White off the Board,
which makes the murder all the more rational.
I know the gay community thinks the murder was anti-gay:
political in that sense. But
I think, they're wrong. Y' know, some people —
in the gay community
— ah — even said I threw the trial.
Before this, I was considered a great friend to the gay community.

Why would I want to throw the trial
— this trial
in an election year?

Oh, there were accusations you wouldn't believe...
At the trial, a woman...
it may have been one of the jurors—
I can't remember...
Actually said—
"But what would Mary Ann White do without her husband?"
And I remember my outrage.
She never thought,
"What will Gina Moscone do without George?"

I must tell you that it's hard for me to talk about a lot of these things,
all of this is just the — just
the tip of the iceberg.

We thought — Tommy and I — Tom Norman and I—
We thought it was an open and shut case
of first degree murder.

(Lights.)

(On screen: THE PSYCHIATRIC DEFENSE)
(Lights up on four psychiatrists in conservative dress, in either separate witness stands or a multiple stand unit.)

NORMAN. It wasn't just an automatic reaction when he fired those last two shots into George Moscone's *brains* was it, Doctor?
COURT. Let's move on Mr. Norman.
You are just arguing with the witnesses now.
NORMAN. Your Honor—
COURT. Let's move on.
SOLOMON. I think he was out of control and in an unreasonable state. And I think if the gun had held, you know, maybe more bullets, maybe he would have shot more bullets. I don't know.
LUNDE. This wasn't just some mild case of the blues.
SOLOMON. I think that, you know, maybe Mr. Moscone would have been just as dead with one bullet. I don't know.
JONES. I think he was out of control.
DELMAN. Yes.
NORMAN. George Moscone was shot four times, Doctor. The gun had five cartridges in it. Does that change your opinion in any way?
SOLOMON. No. I think he just kept shooting for awhile.

(NORMAN throws his notes down.)

SCHMIDT. Now, there is another legal term we deal with in the courtroom, and that is variously called "malice" or "malice aforethought"...? And this must be present in order to convict for murder in the first degree.

JONES. Okay, let me preface this by saying I am not sure how malice is defined. I'll give you what my understanding is. In order to have malice, you would have to be able to do certain things: to be able to be intent to kill somebody unlawfully. You would have to be able to do something for a base and anti-social purpose. You would have to be aware of the duty imposed on you not to do that, not to unlawfully kill somebody or do something for a base, anti-social purpose, that involved a risk of death, and you would have to be able to act, despite having that awareness of that, that you are not supposed to do that, and so you would have to know that you were not supposed to do it, and then also act despite — keeping in mind that you are not supposed to do it. Is that your answer — your question?

SCHMIDT. I think so.

JONES. *(laughs)* I felt that he had the capacity
to do the first three:
that he had the capacity to intend to kill,
but that doesn't take much, you know,
to try to kill somebody,
it's not a high-falutin' mental state.
I think he had the capacity to do something
for a base and anti-social purpose.
I think he had the capacity to know that there was a duty
imposed on him not to do that,
but *I don't think he had the capacity to hold that notion*
in his mind while he was acting;
so that I think that the depression,
plus the moment, the tremendous emotions of the moment, with the depression,

reduced his capacity for conforming conduct.
In fact, I asked him:
"Why didn't you hit them?"
And he was flabbergasted that I asked such a thing,
because it was contrary to his code of behavior,
you know, he was taken aback, kind of—
hit them seemed ridiculous to him—
because it would have been so unfair,
since he could have defeated them so easily
in a fist fight.

SCHMIDT. Thank you. *(HE sits. To NORMAN.)* You may examine.

*[NORMAN. Doctor Jones, when let off at City Hall the accused was let off at the Polk Street entrance and then walked a block and a half to Van Ness Avenue. Why wouldn't he just enter City Hall through the main entrance?

JONES. He got towards the top of the stairs, then looked up, saw the metal detector and thought: "Oh, my goodness, I got that gun."

NORMAN. Doctor, why would he care whether there was a metal detector there, and that a gun would have been discovered upon his person?

JONES. Well, I would presume that would mean some degree of hassle. I mean, I presume that the metal detector would see if somebody is trying to bring a weapon in.

NORMAN. That is usually why they have it. Did he realize at that time that he was unlawfully carrying a concealable firearm?

JONES. I presume so.]

* NOTE: The bracketed section was cut in the Broadway production.

NORMAN. Dr. Jones, if it's a fact that Dan White shot George Moscone twice in the body, and that when George Moscone'fell to the floor disable, he shot twice more into the right side of George Moscone's head at a distance of between 12 and 18 inches, he made a decision at that time, didn't he, to either discharge the gun into the head of George Moscone, or not discharge the gun into the head of George Moscone?

JONES. If decision means he behaved in that way, then, yes.

NORMAN. Well, didn't he have to make some kind of choice based upon some reasoning process?

JONES. Oh, no, not based on reasoning necessarily. I think — I don't think that I — you know, great emotional turmoil in context of major mood disorder — he was enraged and anxious and frustrated in addition to the underlying depression. I think that after Moscone says "How's your family?" or, "What's your wife going to do?" at that point, I think that it's — it's over.

NORMAN. It's over for George Moscone.

SOLOMON. I think that if you look at the gun as a transitional object, you can see that transitional objects are clung to in — in situations of great — of anxiety and insecurity, as one sees with children..

(COURT — raises eyes, gives up.)

NORMAN. Doctor, are you telling us that a person who has lived an otherwise law-abiding life and an otherwise moral life could not premeditate and deliberate as is contemplated by the definition of first degree murder?!

SOLOMON. I'm not saying that absolutely. Obviously, it's more difficult for a person who lives a highly moral life. And this individual, Dan White, had, if you want — a hypertrophy complex. Hypertrophy meaning overdeveloped, morally, rigidly, overdeveloped. In fact, if Mr. White were to receive a light sentence I think there is a distinct possiblity he could take his own life.
But I would say in general, yes.
I don't think you'd kill Mr. Schmidt if you lost this case.

NORMAN. It's unlikely.

SOLOMON. You may be very angry, but I do't think you will do it because I think your are probably a very moral and law abiding citizen, and I think if you did it, I would certainly recommend a psychiatric examination, because I think there would be a serious possibility that you had flipped.

(pause)

It's most interesting to me how split off his feelings were at this time.

LUNDE. Dan White had classical symptoms that are described in diagnostic manuals for depression and, of course, he had characteristics of compulsive personality, which happens to be kind of a bad combination in those sorts of people.

NORMAN. *(frustrated)* Dr. Solomon you are aware that he took a gun with him when he determined to see George Moscone, a loaded gun?

ACT II   EXECUTION OF JUSTICE   77

SOLOMON. Yes.

NORMAN. Why did he take that gun, in your opinion, Dr. Solomon?

SOLOMON. I might say that I think there are symbolic aspects to this.

NORMAN. Symbolic aspects, now Doctor...

COURT. Let's move onto another question.

NORMAN. Well, Your Honor...

COURT. Let's move on.

NORMAN. *(frustrated)* All right. Dr. Delman, after he went in the building armed with a gun through a window and went up to see George Moscone, at the time he came in to see George Moscone, do you feel that he was angry with George Moscone?

DELMAN. Yes.

NORMAN. When George Moscone told him that he wasn't going to appoint him, do you think that that brought about and increased any more anger?

DELMAN. Yes.

NORMAN. All right. Now there was some point in there when he shot George Moscone, isn't that true?

DELMAN. Yes.

NORMAN. Do you know how many times he shot him?

DELMAN. I believe it's four.

NORMAN. Well, Doctor, do you put any significance upon the circumstances that he shot George Moscone twice in the head?

DELMAN. The question is, "Do I put any significance in it?"

NORMAN. Yes.

DELMAN. I really have no idea why that happened.

NORMAN. Well, Doctor, do you think he knew that if you shot a man twice in the head that it was likely to surely kill him?!

DELMAN. I'm sure that he knew that shooting a man in the head would kill him, Mr. Norman.

NORMAN. Thank you! *(HE sits.)*

SCHMIDT. But, it is your conclusion, Doctor, that Dan White could not premeditate or deliberate, within the meaning we have discussed here, on November 27th, 1978?

DELMAN. That is correct.

(NORMAN slaps hands to head.)
(BLINDER enters.)

SCHMIDT. Thank you.
BLINDER. I teach forensic psychiatry.
I teach about the uses and abuses
of psychiatry in the judicial system.
The courts tend to place psychiatry in a position
where it doesn't belong. Where it becomes the sole arbiter
between guilt and innocence.
There is also a tendency in the stresses of the adversary system
to polarize psychiatric testimony so that a psychiatrist finds himself trying to put labels on normal stressful behavior,
and *everything* becomes a mental illness.

And I think that is an abuse.

(He refers to his notes.)

Dan White found City Hall rife of corruption.
With the possible exceptions of Diane Feinstein and Harvey Milk,
the supervisors seemed to make their judgments, their votes,
on the basis of what was good for them,
rather than what was good for the City.

And this was a very frustrating thing for Mr. White:
to want to do a good job for his constituents
and find he was continually defeated.

In addition to these stresses, there were
attacks by the press
and there were threats of literal attacks on Supervisors.
He told me a number of Supervisors like himself
carried a gun to scheduled meetings.
Never any relief from these tensions.

Whenever he felt things were not going right,
He would abandon his usual program of exercise and good nutrition
and start gorging himself on junk foods:
Twinkies, Coca-Cola.

Soon Mr. White was just sitting in front of the TV.
Ordinarily, he reads. (Mr. White has always been an identifiable Jack London adventurer.)

But now, getting very depressed about the fact he would not be reappointed,
he just sat there before the TV
binging on Twinkies.

(On screen: The Twinkie Defense.)

He couldn't sleep.
He was tossing and turning on the couch in the living room
so he wouldn't disturb his wife on the bed.

Virtually no sexual contact at this time.
He was dazed, confused, had crying spells,
became increasingly ill,
and wanted to be left alone.

He told his wife:
"Don't bother cooking any food for me.
I will just munch on these potato chips."

Mr. White stopped shaving and refused to go.
out of the house to help Denise rally support.

He started to receive information that he would not be reappointed
from unlikely sources.

This was very stressing to him.

Again, it got to be cupcakes, candy bars.
He watched the sun come up on Monday morning.

Finally, at 9:00 Denise called.
He decides to go down to City Hall.
He shaves and puts on his suit.
He sees his gun — lying on the table.
Ammunition.
He simultaneously puts these in his pocket.
Denise picks him up.
He's feeling anxious about a variety of things.
He's sitting in the car hyperventilating,
blowing on his hands, repeating:
"Let him tell me to my face why he won't reappoint me.
Did he think I can't take it?
I am a man.
I can take it."

He goes down to City Hall, and I sense that time is short
so let me bridge this by saying that as I believe
it has been testified to,
he circumvents the mental (sic) detector,
goes to the side window,
gets an appointment with the Mayor.
The Mayor almost directly tells him,
"I am not going to reappoint you."

The Mayor puts his arm around him saying;
"Let's have a drink.
What are you going to do now, Dan?
Can you get back into the Fire Department?
What about your family?
Can your wife get her job back?
What's going to happen to them now?"

Somehow this inquiry directed to his family struck a nerve.
The Mayor's voice started to fade out and Mr. White felt
"As if I were in a dream."
He started to leave and then inexplicably turned around
and like a reflex
drew his revolver.
He had no idea how many shots he fired.

The similar event occurred
in Supervisor Milk's office. (sic.)

He remembers being shocked by the sound of the gun.
going off for the second time like a cannon.

He tells me that he was aware he engaged
in a lethal act,
but tells me he gave no thought to his wrongfulness.
As he put it to me:
"I had no chance to even think about it."

He remembers running out of the building
driving, I think, to church,
making arrangements to meet his wife,
and then going from the church
to the Police Department.

(Pause.)
(Exhausted.)

SCHMIDT. Doctor, you have mentioned the ingestion of sugar and sweets and that sort of thing. There are certain theories with regard to sugar and sweets and the ingestion thereof, and I'd like to just touch on that briefly with the jury. Does that have any significance, or could it possibly have any significance?

BLINDER. *(Turns to jury.)* First, there is a substantial body of evidence that in susceptible individuals, large quantities of what we call junk food, high sugar content food with lots of preservatives, can precipitate anti-social and even violent behavior.

There have been studies, for example, where they have taken so-called career criminals and taken them off all their junk food and put them on meat and potatoes and their criminal records immediately evaporate.
(Pause.)
It's contradictory and ironic, but the way it works is that for such a person, the American Dream is a Nightmare. For somebody like Dan White.

SCHMIDT. Thank you, Doctor.

(Lights fade on psychiatrists.)
(Pause.)
(Lights up on MARY ANN WHITE, blazing white She is almost blinded.) (She comes forward.)

SCHMIDT. You are married to that man, is that correct?

MARY ANN. Yes.

SCHMIDT. When did you first meet him?

MARY ANN. I met him *(WITNESS sobbing.)*

SCHMIDT. If you want to take any time// just let us know.

MARY ANN. *(Pulling herself together.)* I met him in April, 1976...

SCHMIDT. And you were married// and you took a trip?

MARY ANN. Yes. Yes, we went to Ireland on our honeymoon because Danny just had this feeling that Ireland could be this place could be really peaceful for him. He just really likes — loves — everything about Ireland and so we — *(sobbing)*

SCHMIDT. Excuse me.

MARY ANN. —so we went there// for about five wee—

SCHMIDT. During that period did you notice anything// unusual about his behavior?

MARY ANN. Yes, I mean, you know, when we went I thought — went thinking it was going to kind of romantic, and when we got there, the thing that attracted me

(NOTE: //=Overlap ... Next speaker starts, first speaker continues.)

most to Danny was his vitality, energy and the fact that he always had the ability to inspire in you something that made you want to do your best like he did, and when we got there, when we got to Ireland...it was all of a sudden, he went into like a two-week long mood, like I had seen before, but I had never seen one, I guess, all the way through, because when we were going out, I might see him for a day, and being a fireman, he would work a day, and then I wouldn't see him, and when we got to Ireland...I mean, I was just newly married and I thought: "What did I do?"

SCHMIDT. After he was on the Board, did you notice these moods// become more frequent?

MARY ANN. Yes, he had talked to me about how hard the job was on him. You know, from June he started to talk about how it was. Obviously you can sense when you are not sleeping together, and you are not really growing together and he would say, "Well, I can't — I can't really think of anyone else when I don't even like myself." And I said, "It's just him. He's not satisfied with what I'm doing and I don't like myself// and so I can't..."

SCHMIDT. Did you see him on the morning of... November 27th?

MARY ANN. Yes// I did.

SCHMIDT. And at that time did he indicate what he was going to do// that day?

MARY ANN. It was just, he was going to stay *home*. He wasn't leaving the house.

SCHMIDT. Later that morning, did you receive a call//to meet him somewhere?

MARY ANN. Yes. I did. Yes, I went to St. Mary's Cathed-

ral. I went and saw him.
I could see that he had been crying, and I, I
just kind of looked at him
and he just looked at me
and he said,
he said,
"I shot the Mayor and Harvey."

SCHMIDT. *(Looks to NORMAN as if to say, "Any questions?" NORMAN nods no.)* Thank you.

(DAN WHITE sobs.)
(SCHMIDT puts hand on WHITE's shoulder.)
*(MARY ANN WHITE stumbles off the stand
to her husband.)*
(WHITE shields his eyes.)
(She looks as if she will embrace him.)

SCHMIDT. The defense is prepared to rest at this time.

(MARY ANN WHITE sobs.)
*(Hyperreal sound of a woman's high heels
on marble echoing.)*
(Mumbled "Hail Mary's.")

COURT. Let me admonish you, ladies gentlemen of the jury, not to discuss this case among yourselves nor with anyone else, not to allow anyone to speak to you about the case, nor are you to form or express an opinion until the matter has been submitted to you.

ACT II   EXECUTION OF JUSTICE

(Gavel.)
(On screen: The Defense rests)
(ALL exit.)

   MILK'S FRIEND. *(Enters alone.)* *We got back from the airport the night of the 27th
And my roommate said;
There's going to be a candle-light march.
By now, we thought it had to have reached City Hall.
So we went directly there. From the airport to City Hall.
And there were maybe 75 people there.
And I remember thinking;
My God is this all anybody...cared?
Somebody said: No, the march hasn't gotten here yet.
So we then walked over to Market Street
which was 2 or 3 blocks away.
And looked down it.
And Market Street runs in a straight line
out to the Castro area.
And as we turned the corner,

*(On screen: The screens flooded with
candles and the candle-light march
music. Barber's "Adagio.")*

there were people as wide as this wide street

---

*Dialogue from *The Times of Harvey Milk*, a film by Robert Epstein and Richard Schmeichen.

As far as you could see.

(The entire company enters holding candles.)
(After awhile.)

YOUNG MOTHER. *Thousands and thousands of people,
And that feeling of such loss.

(Music continues.)

GWENN. *It was one of the most eloquent expressions of a
community's response to violence
that I have ever seen...
A MOURNER. *(Wearing a black arm band.)* I'd like to read from the transcript of Harvey Milk's political will.
(reads)
This is Harvey Milk speaking on Friday, November 18.
This tape is to be played only in the event of my death
by assassination.

(On screen: Pictures of MILK.)

I've given long and considerable thought to this,
and not just since the election.
I've been thinking about this for some time

---

*Dialogue from *The Times of Harvey Milk*, a film by Robert Epstein and Richard Schmeichen.

prior to the election and certainly over the years.
I fully realize that a person who stands for what I stand for—
a gay activist—
becomes the target for a person who is insecure, terrified,
afraid or very disturbed themselves.

(DAN WHITE enters. Stops.)

Knowing that I could be assassinated at any moment
or any time,
I feel it's important that some people should understand
my thoughts.
So the following are my thoughts, my wishes, my desires,
I'd like to pass them on and have them played for the appropriate people.
The first and most obvious concern is that
if I was to be shot and killed,
the mayor has the power,
George Moscone.

*(On screen: Pictures of MOSCONE, the
funeral, the mourners, the widow.)*

of appointing my successor...
to the Board of Supervisors.
I cannot prevent some people
from feeling angry and frustrated and mad,

but I hope
that they would not demonstrate violently.
If a bullet should enter my brain,
let that bullet destroy every closet door.

(Gavel.)
(All MOURNERS blow out candles.)
(DAN WHITE sits.)
(Blackout.)

(On screen: The People's rebuttal/Dr. Levy Psychiatrist)
(Lights up.)

LEVY. I interviewed the defendant several hours after
the shootings of November 27th.
In my opinion, one can get a more accurate diagnosis
the closer one examines the suspect
after a crime has been committed.
At that time, it appeared to me that Dan White had
no remorse for the death of George Moscone.
It appeared to me, he had no remorse
for the death of Harvey Milk.
There was nothing in my interview which would suggest
to me
there was any mental disorder.
I had the feeling that there was some depression
but it was not
depression that I would consider as a diagnosis.

In fact, I found him to be less depressed
than I would have expected him to be.
At that time I saw him, it seemed that he felt himself
to be quite justified.
(Looks to notes.)
I felt he had the capacity to form malice.
I felt he had the capacity to premeditate. And...
I felt he had the capacity to deliberate, to arrive at a
course of conduct weighing considerations.

NORMAN. Did you review the transcript of the proceeding wherein the testimonies of Drs. Jones, Blinder, Solomon, Delman and Lunde were given?

LEVY. Yes. I found nothing in them that would cause me to revise my opinion.

NORMAN. Thank you, Dr. Levy. *(sits)*

(SCHMIDT stands.)

SCHMIDT. Dr. Levy, are you a full professor at the University of California?

LEVY. No. I am an associate clinical professor.

(SCHMIDT smiles, looks to jury.)

SCHMIDT. May I inquire of your age, sir?
LEVY. I'm 55.
SCHMIDT. Huh. *(Picking up papers.)* Doctor, your report is dated November 27, 1978, is it not?
LEVY. Yes.

SCHMIDT. And yet the report was not written on November 27, 1978?

LEVY. No. It would have been within several days// of that time.

SCHMIDT. And then it was dated November 27, 1978?

LEVY. Yes.

SCHMIDT. Well, regardless of the backdating, or whatever, when did you come to your forensic conclusions?

LEVY. I'd say the conslusions would have been on November 27th.

SCHMIDT. And that was after a two-hour talk with Dan White?

LEVY. Yes.

SCHMIDT. Doctor, would it be fair to say that you made some snap decisions?

LEVY. I don't believe// I did.

SCHMIDT. Did you consult with any other doctors?

LEVY. No.

SCHMIDT. Did you review any of the witnesses' statements?

LEVY. No.

SCHMIDT. Did you consult any of the material that was available to you, save and except for the tape of Dan White on the same date?

LEVY. No. That was all that was made available to me// at that time.

SCHMIDT. Now I don't mean to be facetious, but this is a fairly important case, is that fair?

LEVY. I would certainly think so,// yes.

SCHMIDT. But you didn't talk further with Mr. white?
LEVY. No. I was not requested to.
SCHMIDT. And you didn't request to talk to him further?
LEVY. No. I was not going to do a complete assessment.
SCHMIDT. Well, in fact, you didn't do a complete assessment, is that fair?
LEVY. I was not asked to do a complete assessment.
COURT. Doctor, you are fading away.
LEVY. *I was not asked to do a complete assessment.*
SCHMIDT. Thank you.

(Blackout.)
*(Commotion in court, JOANNA tries to
get interview from LEVY.)*

SCHMIDT. *(In black.)* She wants to tell the story so it's not
responsive to the questions.

(Lights up.)
*(On screen: SUPERVISOR CAROL RUTH SILVER,
for the prosecution.)*

SILVER. *(Very agitated, speaking fast, heated.)*
The prosecution asked in what other case did a dispute between Dan White and Harvey Milk arise! And it was the Polk Street closing was another occasion when Harvey requested that Polk Street, which is a heavily gay area

in San Francisco, I am sure everybody knows, and on Halloween had traditionally had a huge number of people in costumes and so forth down there and has// traditionally been recommended for closure by the Police Department and—

SCHMIDT. I am going to object to this, Your Honor.

SILVER. It was recommended—

COURT. Just ask the next question. Just ask the next question.

SILVER. I am sorry.

NORMAN. Did Mr.Milk and Mr. White take positions that were opposite to each other?

SILVER. Yes.

NORMAN. Was there anything that became, well, rather loud and perhaps hostile in connection or consisting between the two?

SILVER. Not loud but very hostile
You have to first understand that this street closure was recommended by the Police Chief and had been
done customarily in the years past// and is, was —came up as a uncontested issue practically.

SCHMIDT. Your Honor, I again—

COURT. Please, just make your objection.

SCHMIDT. I'd like to.

COURT. Without going through contortions.

SCHMIDT. There is an objection.

COURT. All right. Sustained.

NORMAN. Miss Silver, did you know, or did you ever see Mr. White to appear to be depressed or to be

withdrawn?
SILVER. No.
NORMAN. Thank you. *(sits)*

(SILVER flabbergasted, upset.)

COURT. All right. Any questions, Mr. Schmidt?
SCHMIDT. Is it *Miss* Silver?
SILVER. Yes.
SCHMIDT. Miss Silver, you never had lunch with Dan White, did you?
SILVER. Did I ever have lunch?

(Subliminal music.)

NOTHENBERG. George Moscone was socially brilliant in that he could find the injustice.
SCHMIDT. I mean the two of you?
SILVER. I don't recall having done so// but I—
NOTHENBERG. His mind went immediately to what can we do?
SCHMIDT. Did you socialize frequently?
NOTHENBERG. What can we practically do?
SILVER. No, when his son was born// I went to a party at his house and that kind of thing.
SCHMIDT. Did Mr. Norman contact you last week, or did you// contact him?
NOTHENBERG. I was with George registering voters in Mississippi in 1964.

SILVER. On Friday morning I called his office.

NOTHENBERG. Y'know, he'd never seen that kind of despair before, but when he saw it he said right out: "This is intolerable."

SILVER. because I was reading the newspaper—

SCHMIDT. Yes.

SILVER. And it appeared// to me that—

COURT. Don't tell us.

NOTHENBERG. And whenever he said: "this is *intolerable*,"

SILVER. I'm sorry.

NOTHENBERG. In all the years I knew him, he always *did* something about it.

COURT. The jurors are told not to read the newspaper, and I am hoping that they haven't// read the newspapers.

SILVER. I apologize.

COURT. Okay.

SCHMIDT. Miss Silver—

COURT. I am sorry, I didn't want to cut her off—

SILVER. No, I understand.

COURT. from any other answer

SCHMIDT. I think she did complete the answer, Judge.
In any event, you contacted Mr. Norman, did you not?

SILVER. Yes, I did.

SCHMIDT. And at that time, you offered to Mr. Norman to round up people who could say that Dan White never looked depressed at City Hall, is that fair?

SILVER. That's right. Well, I offered to testify to that effect and I suggested that there were other people// who could similarly testify to that fact.

SCHMIDT. In fact, you expressed it though you haven't sat here and listened to the testimony in this courtroom?

SILVER. No, I have never been here before Friday when I was subpeonaed// and spent some time in the jury room.

SCHMIDT. But to use your words, after having read what was in the paper, you said that the defense sounded like "bullshit" to you? That's correct.

DENMAN. I thought I would be a chief witness for the prosecution.

SCHMIDT. Would that suggest then that perhaps you have a bias in this case?

DENMAN. What was left unsaid was what the trial should have been about.

SILVER. I certainly have a bias.

SCHMIDT. You are a political enemy of Dan White's is that fair?

SILVER. No, that's not true.

DENMAN. Before, y'know, there was a lot of talk about assassinating the Mayor among thuggish elements of the Police Officers Association.

SCHMIDT. Did you have any training in psychology or psychiatry?

DENMAN. And those were the cops Dan White was closest to.

SILVER. No more than some of the kind of C.E.B. courses// lawyer's psychology for lawyers kind of training.

DENMAN. I think he knew a lot of guys would think he did the right thing and yeah they would make him a hero.

SCHMIDT. I mean, would you be able to diagnois, say, *Manic depression depressed type,* or could you distinguish that from *uni-polar depression?*

SILVER. No.

DENMAN. I was Dan White's jailer for 72 hours after the assassinations.

SCHMIDT. Did you ever talk to him about his dietary habits or anything like that?

DENMAN. There were no tears.

SILVER. I remember a conversation about nutrition or something like that. but I can't remember// the substance of it.

SCHMIDT. I don't have anything further.

DENMAN. There was no shame.

COURT. Any redirect, Mr. Norman?

NORMAN. Yes.

DENMAN. You got the feeling that he knew exactly what he was doing and there was no remorse.

NORMAN. Miss Silver, you were asked if you had a bias in this case. You knew Harvey Milk very well and you liked him, didn't you?

SILVER. I did; and also George Moscone.

NORMAN. Miss Silver, speaking of a bias, had you ever heard the Defendant say anything about getting people of whom Harvey Milk numbered himself?

(Lights up on MILK's friend.)

SILVER. In the Polk Street debate—

MILK'S FRIEND. The night Harvey was elected, I went to bed early because it was more happiness that I had been taught to deal with.

SILVER. Dan White got up and gave—
a long diatribe—

MILK'S FRIEND. Next morning we put up signs saying "thank you."

SILVER. Just a — a very unexpected and very uncharacteristic of Dan, long hostile speech about how gays and their lifestyles had to be contained and we can't//
encourage this kind of thing and—

SCHMIDT. I am going to object to this, your Honor.

COURT. Sustained, okay.

MILK'S FRIEND. During that, Harvey came over and told me
that he had made a political will
because he expected he'd be killed.
And then in the same breath, he said (I'll never forget it):
"It works, it works..."

NORMAN. All right...that's all.

MILK'S FRIEND. The system works// ...

NORMAN. Thank you.

DENMAN. When White was being booked, it all seemed fraternal. One officer gave Dan a pat on the behind when he was booked, sort of a "Hey, catch you later, Dan," pat.

COURT. Any recross?

DENMAN. Some of the officers and deputies were standing around with half-smirks on their faces. Some were actually laughing.
SCHMIDT. Just a couple.
DENMAN. The joke they kept telling was,
"Dan White's mother says to him when he comes home,
'No, dummy, I said milk and baloney, not Moscone!' "
(pause)
SCHMIDT. Miss Silver, you are a part of the gay community also, are you?
SILVER. Myself?
SCHMIDT. Yes.
SILVER. You mean, am I gay?
SCHMIDT. Yes.
SILVER. No, I'm not.
SCHMIDT. I have nothing further.
MOSCONE'S FRIEND. George would have said, "This is intolerable," and he'd have done something about it.
COURT. All right, Miss Silver you may leave.
COURT. Next witness, please.

(Lights.)
(SILVER exits towards door.)
(JOANNA with TV lights.)

JOANNA LU. Miss Silver, Supervisor Silver, would you like to elaborate on Mr. White's anti-gay feelings or hostility to Harvey Milk or George Moscone?
SILVER. No comment, right now.

(SILVER distraught, rushes past.)

JOANNA LU. Did you feel you were baited, did you have your say?
SILVER. *(Blows up.)* I said I have no comment at this time!!!

(She exits.)

COURT. Mr. Norman? Next witness?
NORMAN. Nothing further.
Those are all the witnesses we have to present.
COURT. The People rest?
NORMAN. Yes.
COURT. Does the defense have any witnesses?
SCHMIDT. *(surprised)* Well, we can discuss it, Your Honor. I am not sure there is anything to rebut.

(Light change.)
(Commontion in court.)
(On screen: The People Rest)
(Lights up on SCHMIDT.)
*(He is at a podium, a parish priest
at a pulpit.)*
(Dissolve to on screen: Summations)

SCHMIDT. I'm nervous. I'm very nervous. I sure hope I say all the right things. I can't marshal words the way Mr. Norman can — but — I believe strongly in things.

Lord God! I don't say to you to forgive Dan White. I don't say to you to just let Dan White walk out of here a free man. He is guilty. But, the degree of responsibility is the issue here. The state of mind is the issue here. It's not who was killed; it's why. It's not who killed them; but why. The state of mind is the issue here.

Lord God! The pressures.
Nobody can say that the things that happened to him days
or weeks preceeding wouldn't make a reasonable and ordinary man
at least mad,
angry in some way.

Surely — surely, that had to have arisen, not to kill,
not to kill, just to be mad, to act irrationally,
because if you kill, when you are angry, or under the heat of passion,
if you kill, then the law will punish you,
and you will be punished by God—
God will punish you,
but the law will also punish you.

Heat of passion fogs judgement, makes one act irrationally,
in the very least,
and my God,
that is what happened at the very least.

Forget about the mental illness,
forget about all the rest of the factors
that came into play at the same time;
Surely he acted irrationally, impulsively — out of
  some passion.

Now...you will recall at the close of the prosecution's
  case,
it was suggested to you this was a calm, cool, delib-
  erating,
terrible terrible person
that had committed two crimes like these,
and these are terrible crimes,
and that he was emotionally stable at that time
and there wasn't anything wrong with him.

He didn't have any diminished capacity.
Then we played these tapes he made directly after
he turned himself in at Northern Station.

My God,
that was not a person that was calm and collected and
  cool
and able to weigh things out.
It just wasn't.

The tape just totally fogged me up the first time I
  heard it.
It was a man that was, as Frank Falzon said, broken.
Shattered.

This was not the Dan White that everybody had known.

Something happened to him and he snapped.
That's the word I used in my opening statement.
Something snapped here.

The pot had boiled over here,
and people that boil over in that fashion,
they tell the truth.

Have the tape played again, if you can't remember what was said.
He said in no uncertain terms,

"My God,
why did I do these things?
What made me do this?
How on earth could I have done this?
I didn't intend to hurt anybody.
My God,
what happened to me?
Why?"

Play the tape.
If everybody says the tape is truthful, play the tape.
I'd agree it's truthful.

With regard to the reloading and some of these little discrepancies that appeared to come up.
I am not even sure of the discrepancies,

but if there were discrepancies,
listen to it in context.
"Where did you reload?"
"I reloaded in my office, I think."
"And then did you leave the Mayor's office?"
"Yes, then I left the Mayor's office."

That doesn't mean anything to me at all.
It doesn't mean anything to me at all.
And I don't care where the reloading took place!

But listen to the tape.
It says in no uncertain terms,
"I didn't intend to hurt anybody.
I didn't intend to do this.
Why do we do things?

I don't know.
It was a man desperately trying to grab at something...

"What happened to me?
How could I have done this?"

If the District Attorney concedes that what is
on the tape is truthful,
and I believe that's the insinuation we have here,
then, by golly,
there is voluntary manslaughter,
nothing more and nothing less. I say this to you in all honesty.

And if you have any doubts our law tells you,
you have to judge in favor of Dan White.

Now, I don't know what more I can say.
He's got to be punished
and he will be punished.
He's going to have to live with this for the rest of his life.
His child will live with it
and his family will live with it
and God will punish him
and the law will punish him,
and they will punish him severely.
And this is the type of case where, I suppose
I don't think Mr. Norman will do it
but you can make up a picture of a dead man
or two of them for that matter
and you can have them around and say
somebody is going to pay for this
and somebody *is* going to pay for this.
But it's not an emotional type thing.
I get emotional about it
but *you* can't
because you have to be objective about the facts.

But please, please
Just justice.
That's all.
Just justice here.

(SCHMIDT appears to break for a moment.)

Now I get one argument.
I have made it.
And I just hope that—
I just hope that you'll come to the same
   conclusion
that I have come to,
and thank you for listening to me.
   NORMAN. Ladies and gentlemen,
I listened very carefully to the summation just given
   you.
It appears to me, members of the jury,
to be a very facile explanation and rationalization
as to premediation and deliberation.
The evidence that has been laid before you
screams for murder in the first degree.

What counsel for the defense has done is suggest to
   you
to *excuse* this kind of conduct and call it something that
it isn't,
to call it voluntary manslughter.

Members of the jury, you are the triers of fact here.
You have been asked to hear this tape recording
   again.
The tape recording has been aptly described
as something very moving. We all feel a sense of
   sympathy,
a sense of empathy for our fellow man, but you are not
   to let

sympathy influence you in your judgment.

To reduce the charge of murder to something less—
to reduce it to voluntary manslaughter—
means you are saying that this was not murder.
That this was an intentional killing of a human being
upon a quarrel, or heat of passion.
But ladies and gentlemen,
that quarrel must have been so extreme,
at the time
that the defendant could not—
was incapable of forming
those qualities of thought which are
malice, premeditation and deliberation.
But the evidence in this case doesn't suggest that at all.
Not at all.
If the defendant had picked up a vase or something
that happened to be in the mayor's ofice
and hit the mayor over the head and killed him
you know, you know that argument for voluntary manslaughter
might be one which you could say the evidence admits
a reasonable doubt. But—

Ladies and gentlemen:
THE FACTS ARE:
It was *he* — Dan White — who brought the gun to the City Hall
The gun was not there.

It was *he* who brought the extra cartidges for the gun;
they were not found there

He went to City Hall and when he got there he went
to the Polk Street door.

There was a metal detector there.
He knew he was carrying a gun.
He knew that he had extra cartidges for it.

Instead of going through the metal detector,
he *decided* to go around the corner.
He was capable at that time of expressing anger.
He was capable of, according to the doctor—
well, parenthetically, members of the jury,
I don't know how they can look in your head and tell you
what you are able to do. But—
They even said that he was capable of knowing at that time
that if you pointed a gun at somebody and you fired that gun
that you would surely kill a person.

He went around the corner, and climbed
through a window into City Hall.

He went up to the Mayor's office.
He appeared, according to witnesses,
to act calmly in his approach, in his speech.

He chatted with Cyr Copertini; he was capable of
carrying on a conversation to the extent that he was
able to ask her how she was, after having asked to see
the Mayor.

(Looks to audience.)

He stepped into the Mayor's office.
After some conversation,

he shot the Mayor twice in the body.
Then he shot the Mayor in the head twice
while the Mayor was disabled on the floor.
The evidence suggests that in order to shoot the Mayor
twice in the head
he had to *lean down* to do it.

(And NORMAN does.)
(Looks to jury.)

Deliberation is premeditation.
It has malice.
I feel stultified to even bring this up.
This is the definition of murder.

He reloaded the gun.
Wherever he reloaded the gun, it was *he* who
reloaded it!

He did see Supervisor Milk

whom he knew was acting against his appointment
and he was capable of expressing anger in that regard.

He entered the Supervisor's area (a block from the Mayor's
office across City Hall)
and was told, "Dianne wants to see you."
He said, "That is going to have to wait a moment.
I have something to do first."

Then he walked to Harvey Milk's office, put his head in the door and said
"Can I see you a moment, Harv?"
The reply was. "Yes."

He went across the hall and put three bullets
into Harvey Milk's body,
one of which hit Harvey directly in the back.
When he fell to the floor disabled,
two more were delivered to the back of his head.

Now what do you call that but premeditation and deliberation?
What do you call that realistically
but a cold-blooded killing?
Two *cold-blooded executions.*
It occurs to me that if you don't call them that,
then you are ignoring the objective evidence
and the objective facts here.

Members of the jury, there are circumstances here
which no doubt bring about anger,
maybe even rage, I don't know,
but the manner in which that anger was felt
and was handled
is *socially something that cannot be approved.*

Ladies and gentlemen,
the quality of your service is reflected in your verdict.

(He sits.)
*(JOANNA LU at door
stops SCHMIDT. TV lights.)*

JOANNA LU. Mr. Schmidt, do you
SCHMIDT. Yes.
JOANNA LU. Do you feel society would feel justice is served if the jury returns two manslaughter verdicts?
SCHMIDT. Society doesn't have anything to do with it. Only those 12 people in the jury box.

(Gavel.)

COURT. Ladies and gentlemen of the jury,
Now that you have heard the evidence,
we come to that part of the trial where you are instructed
on the applicable law.

In the crime of murder of the first degree
the necessary concurrent mental states are:
Malice aforethought, premeditation and deliberation.
In the crime of murder of the second degree,

the necessary concurrent mental state is:
Malice aforethought.
In the crime of voluntary manslaughter,
the necessary mental state is:
an intent to kill.
Involuntary manslaughter is an unlawful killing
without malice aforethought
and without intent to kill.

The law does not undertake to limit or define
the kinds of passion
which may cause a person to act rashly.
Such passions as desperation,
humiliation, resentment,
anger, fear, or rage
or any other high wrought emotion...
can be sufficient to reduce the killings to manslaughter
so long as they are sufficient
to obscure the reason
and render the average man likely to act rashly.

There is no malice aforethought
if the killing occurred upon a sudden quarrel
or heat of passion.

There is no malice aforethought
if the evidence shows that due to diminished capacity
caused by illness, mental defect, or intoxication,
the defendant did not have the capacity
to form the mental state constituting malice aforethought,
even though the killing was intentional,
voluntary, premeditated and unprovoked.

(A siren begins to cover the court.)
*(On screen: Images of the riot at City
Hall begin to appear.
Broken glass
images of cop cars burning, riot police, angry faces.)*
*(On audio: Explosions
it is the riot.)*

GWENN. *(On video.)* In order to understand the riots, I think you have to understand that the Dan White verdict did not occur in a vacuum—

COURT. Mr. Foreman, has the jury reached verdicts// in this case?

GWENN. that there were and are other factors which contribute to a legitimate rage that was demonstrated dramatically at our symbol of Who's Responsible, City Hall.

*(On screen: Images of City Hall being
stormed.
Line of police in front in riot gear.)*

FOREMAN. Yes, it has, Your Honor.
GWENN. The verdict came down and the people rioted.
COURT. Please read the verdicts.
GWENN. The people stormed City Hall, burned police cars.

*(On screen: Image of City Hall.
Line of police cars in flames.)*

FOREMAN. *(reading)* The jury finds the defendant Daniel James White guilty of violating Section 192.1 of the penal code,

GWENN. Then the police came into our neighborhood. And the police rioted.

FOREMAN. Voluntary manslaughter, for the slaying of Mayor George Moscone.

(MARY ANN WHITE gasps.)
(DAN WHITE puts head in hands.)
(Explosion.)
(Riot police enter.)

GWENN. The police came into the Castro and assaulted gays.
They stormed the Elephant Walk Bar.
One kid had an epileptic seizure and was almost killed for it.
A cop drove a motorcycle up against a phone booth where a lesbian woman was on the phone.
blocked her exit
and began beating her up.

COURT. Is this a unanimous verdict of the jury?

FOREMAN. Yes, it is, Judge.

GWENN. I want to talk about when people are pushed to the wall. *(Off video.)*

COURT. Will each juror say "yea"// or "nay?"

YOUNG MOTHER. What about the children?

MOSCONE'S FRIEND. I know who George offended.
I know who Harvey offended.

JURORS. Yea, yea, yea// yea, yea, yea.

MOSCONE'S FRIEND. I understand the offense.
YOUNG MOTHER. What do I tell my kids?
GWENN. Were the ones who are responsible seeing these things?
YOUNG MOTHER. That in this country you serve more time for robbing a bank than for killing two people?
JURORS. Yea, yea, yea// yea, yea, yea.
GWENN. Hearing these things?
MILK'S FRIEND. I understand the offense.
GWENN. Do they understand about people being pushed to the wall?
YOUNG MOTHER. Accountability?

(Yea's end.)

MILK'S FRIEND. Assassination.
I've grown up with it.
I forget it hasn't always been this way.
YOUNG MOTHER. What do I say?
That two lives are worth seven years and eight months//
   in jail
MILK'S FRIEND. I remember coming home from school in second grade—
JKF was killed—
Five years later, Martin Luther King.
It's a frame of reference.

(explosion)

COURT. Will the Foreman please read the verdict for the second count?

DENMAN. It's a divided city.

FOREMAN. The jury finds the defendant Daniel James White guilty of violating Section 192.1 of the penal code, voluntary manslaughter,
in the slaying of Supervisor Harvey Milk.

(DAN WHITE gasps.)
(MARY ANN WHITE sobs.)
(NORMAN, flushed, head in hands.)
(Explosion.)
(Violence ends.)
(Riot police do terror control.)
(TV lights.)

BRITT. *(On camera.)* No — I'm optimistic about San Francisco.

COURT. Is this a unanimous decision by the jury?

FOREMAN. Yes, Your Honor.

BRITT. I'm Harry Britt. I was Harvey Milk's successor.

MOSCONE'S FRIEND. If he'd just killed George, he'd be in jail for life.

BRITT. Now this is an example I don't use often because people will misunderstand it, but when a prophet is killed, it's up to those who are left to build the community or the church.

MOSCONE'S FRIEND. Dan White believed in the death// penalty...

YOUNG MOTHER. To this jury Dan White// was their son.

NOTHENBERG. He should have gotten the death penalty.

YOUNG MOTHER. What are we teaching our sons?
BRITT. But I have hope.
MILK'S FRIEND. It was an effective assassination.
BRITT. I have hope. And as Harvey said, "you can't live// without hope."
MILK'S FRIEND. They always are.
BRITT. "And you, and you, and you — we gotta give em hope."

(Riot ends.)

JOANNA LU. *(On camera.)* Dan White was examined by the psychiatrist at the state prison. They decided against therapy. Dan White had no apparent signs of mental disorder...Dan White's parole date was January 6, 1984. When Dan White left Soledad prison on January 6, 1984, it was five years, one month, and eight days since he turned himself in at Northern Station after the assassinations of Mayor George Moscone and Supervisor Milk. Mayor Diane Feinstein, the current Mayor of San Francisco, has tried to keep Dan White out of San Francisco during his parole for fear he will be killed.

BOOM BOOM. *(enters)* Dan White! It's 1984 and Big Sister is watching you.

JOANNA LU. Dan White reportedly plans to move to Ireland after his release.

NOTHENBERG. What do you do with your feelings of revenge?
With your need for retribution?

BRITT. We will never forget.

(Riot images freeze.)

BOOM BOOM. *(enters)* I would like to close with a reading from the Book of Dan. *(Opens book.)* Take of this and eat, for this is my defense. *(Raises the Twinkie. Eats it. Exits.)*

JOANNA LU. Dan White was found dead of carbon monoxide poisoning on October 21, 1985, at his wife's home in San Francisco, California.

(Lights change.)
(DAN WHITE faces the court.)

COURT. Mr. White, you are sentenced to seven years and eight months, the maximum sentence for these two counts of voluntary manslaughter. The Court feels that these sentences for the taking of life is completely inappropriate but that was the decision of the legislature.
Again, let me repeat for the record:
Seven years and eight months is the maximum sentence for
voluntary manslaughter, and this is the law.

(Gavel.)
(Long pause.)
(WHITE turns to the audience/jury.)

DAN WHITE. I was always just a lonely vote on the board.
I was just trying to do a good job for the city.

(Long pause.)

*(Audio: Hyperreal sounds of a woman's
high heels on marble.)*
*(Mumbled Hail Mary's. Rustle of an
embrace.)*
(SISTER BOOM BOOM enters. Taunts police.)
(Police raise riot shields.)
(Blackout.)
(On screen: Execution of justice)
(Gavel echoes.)
(END OF PLAY)